De Anima

ARISTOTLE

TRANSLATED BY R.D. HICKS

COSIMOCLASSICS

NEW YORK

Knowledge, however, is an attribute of the soul, and so are perception, opinion, desire, wish, and appetency generally; animal locomotion also is produced
by the soul; and likewise growth, maturity, and decay. Shall we then say that
each of these belongs to the whole soul, that we think, that is, and perceive and
are moved and in each of the other operations act and are acted upon with the
whole soul, or that the different operations are to be assigned to different parts?

—from Book I

BOOK I

1. Cognition is in our eyes a thing of beauty and worth, and this is true of one cognition more than another, either because it is exact or because it relates to more important and remarkable objects. On both these grounds we may with good reason claim a high place for the inquiry concerning the soul. It would seem, too, that an acquaintance with the subject contributes greatly to the whole domain of truth and, more particularly, to the study of nature, the soul being virtually the principle of all animal life.

Our aim is to discover and ascertain the nature and essence of soul and, in the next place, all the accidents belonging to it; of which some are thought to be attributes peculiar to the soul itself, while others, it is held, belong to the animal also, but owe their existence to the soul. But everywhere and in every way it is extremely difficult to arrive at any trustworthy conclusion on the subject. It is the same here as in many other inquiries. What we have to investigate is the essential nature of things and the What.

9

It might therefore be thought that there is a single procedure applicable to all the objects whose essential nature we wish to discover, as demonstration is applicable to the properties which go along with them: in that case we should have to inquire what this procedure is. If, however, there is no single procedure common to all sciences for defining the What, our task becomes still more difficult, as it will then be necessary to settle in each particular case the method to be pursued. Further, even if it be evident that it consists in demonstration of some sort or division or some other procedure, there is still room for much perplexity and error, when we ask from what premisses our inquiry should start, for there are different premisses for different sciences; for the science of numbers, for example, and plane geometry.

402b The first thing necessary is no doubt to determine under which of the summa genera soul comes and what it is; I mean, whether it is a particular thing, i.e. substance, or is quality or is quantity, or falls under any other of the categories already determined. We must further ask whether it is amongst things potentially existent or is rather a sort of actuality, the distinction being all-important. Again, we must consider whether it is divisible or indivisible; whether, again, all and every soul is homogeneous or not; and, if not, whether the difference between the various souls is a difference of species or a difference of genus: for at present discussions and investigations about soul would appear to be restricted to the human soul. We must take care not to overlook the question whether there is a single definition of soul answering to a single definition of animal; or whether there is a different definition for each separate soul, as for horse and dog, man and god: animal, as the universal, being regarded either as nonexistent or, if existent, as logically posterior. This is a question which might equally be raised in regard to any other common predicate. Further, on the assumption that there are not several souls, but merely several different parts in the same soul, it is a question whether we should begin by investigating soul as a whole or its several parts. And here again it is difficult to determine which of these parts are really distinct from one another and whether the several parts, or their functions, should be investigated first. Thus, e.g., should the process of thinking come first or the mind that thinks, the process of sensation or the sensitive faculty? And so everywhere else. But, if the functions should come first, again will arise the question whether we should first investigate the correlative objects. Shall we take, e.g., the sensible object before the faculty of sense and the intelligible object before the intellect?

It would seem that not only is the knowledge of a thing's essential nature useful for discovering the causes of its attributes, as, e.g., in mathematics the knowledge of what is meant by the terms straight or curved, line or surface, aids us in discovering to how many right angles the angles of a triangle are equal: but also, conversely, a knowledge of the attributes is a considerable aid to the knowledge of what a thing is. For when we are able to give an account of all, or at any rate most, of the attributes as they are presented to us, then we shall be in a position to define most exactly the essential nature of the thing. In fact, the starting point of every demonstration is a definition of what something is. Hence the definitions which lead to no information about attributes and do not facilitate even conjecture respecting them have clearly been framed for dialectic and are void of content, one and all.   403a

A further difficulty arises as to whether all attributes of the soul are also shared by that which contains the soul or whether any of them are peculiar to the soul itself: a question which it is indispensable, and yet by no means easy, to decide. It would appear that in most cases soul neither acts nor is acted upon apart from the body: as, e.g., in anger, confidence, desire, and sensation in general. Thought, if anything, would seem to be peculiar to the soul. Yet, if thought is a sort of imagination, or not independent of imagination, it will follow that even thought cannot be independent of the body. If, then, there be any of the functions or affections of the soul peculiar to it, it will be possible for the soul to be separated from the body: if, on the other hand, there is nothing of the sort peculiar to it, the soul will not be capable of separate existence. As with the straight line, so with it. The line, *qua* straight, has many properties; for instance, it touches the brazen sphere at a point; but it by no means follows that it will so touch it if separated. In fact it is inseparable, since it is always conjoined with body of some sort. So, too, the attributes of the soul appear to be all conjoined with body: such attributes, viz., as anger, mildness, fear, pity, courage; also joy, love, and hate; all of which are attended by some particular affection of the body. This indeed is shown by the fact that sometimes violent and palpable incentives occur without producing in us exasperation or fear, while at other times we are moved by slight and scarcely perceptible causes, when the blood is up and the bodily condition that of anger. Still more is this evident from the fact that sometimes even without the occurrence of anything terrible men exhibit all the symptoms of terror. If this be so, the attributes are evidently forms or notions realized in matter. Hence they must be defined accordingly: anger, for instance, as a certain movement in a body of a given kind, or some part or faculty of it, produced by such and such a cause and for such and such an end. These facts at once bring the investigation of soul, whether in its entirety or in the particular aspect described, within the province of the natural philosopher. But every such attribute would be differently defined by the physicist and the dialectician or philosopher. Anger, for instance, would be defined by the dialectician as desire for retaliation or the like, by the physicist as a ferment of the blood or heat which is about the heart: the one of them gives the matter, the other the form or notion. For the notion is the form of the thing, but this notion, if it is to be, must be realized in matter of a particular kind; just as in the case of a house. The notion or definition of a house would be as follows: a shelter to protect us from harm by wind or rain or scorching heat; while another will describe it as stones, bricks, and timber; and again another as the form realized in these materials and subserving given ends. Which then of these is the true physicist? Is it he who confines himself to the matter, while ignoring the form? Or he who treats of the form exclusively? I answer, it is rather he who in his definition takes account of both. What then of each of the other two? Or shall we rather say that there is no one who deals with properties which are not separable nor yet treated as separable, but the physicist deals with all the active properties or passive affections belonging to body of a given sort and the corresponding matter? All attributes not regarded as so belonging he leaves to someone else: who in certain cases is an expert, a carpenter, for instance, or a physician. The attributes which, though inseparable, are not regarded as properties of body of a given sort, but are reached by abstraction, fall within the province of the mathematician: while attributes which are regarded as having separate existence fall to the first philosopher or metaphysician. But to return to the point of digression. We were saying that the attributes of the soul are as such,—I mean, as anger and fear, inseparable from the physical matter of the animals to which they belong, and not, like line and surface, separable in thought.

403b

2. In our inquiry concerning soul it is necessary to state the problems which must be solved as we proceed, and at the same time to collect the views of our predecessors who had anything to say on the subject, in order that we may adopt what is right in their conclusions and guard against their mistakes. Our inquiry will begin by presenting what are commonly held to be in a special degree the natural attributes of soul. Now there are two points especially wherein that which is animate is held to differ from the inanimate, namely, motion and the act of sensation: and these are approximately the two characteristics of soul handed down to us by our predecessors. There are some who maintain that soul is preeminently and primarily the cause of movement. But they imagined that that which is not itself in motion cannot move anything else, and thus they regarded the soul as a thing which is in motion. Hence Democritus affirms the soul to be a sort of fire or heat. For the "shapes" or atoms are infinite and those which are spherical he declares to be fire and soul: they may be compared with the so-called motes in the air, which are seen in the sunbeams that enter through our windows. The aggregate of such seeds, he tells us, forms the constituent elements of the whole of nature (and herein he agrees with Leucippus), while those of them which are spherical form the soul, because such figures most easily find their way through everything and, being themselves in motion, set other things in motion. The atomists assume that it is the soul which imparts motion to animals. It is for this reason that they make life depend upon respiration. For, when the surrounding air presses upon bodies and tends to extrude those atomic shapes which, because they are never at rest themselves, impart motion to animals, then they are reinforced from outside by the entry of other like atoms in respiration, which in fact, by helping to check compression

404a

and solidification, prevent the escape of the atoms already contained in the animals; and life, so they hold, continues so long as there is strength to do this. The doctrine of the Pythagoreans seems also to contain the same thought. Some of them identified soul with the motes in the air, others with that which sets these motes in motion: and as to these motes it has been stated that they are seen to be in incessant motion, even though there be a perfect calm. The view of others who describe the soul as that which moves itself tends in the same direction. For it would seem that all these thinkers regard motion as the most distinctive characteristic of the soul. Everything else, they think, is moved by the soul, but the soul is moved by itself: and this because they never see anything cause motion without itself being in motion. Similarly the soul is said to be the moving principle by Anaxagoras and all others who have held that mind sets the universe in motion; but not altogether in the same sense as by Democritus. The latter, indeed, absolutely identified soul and mind, holding that the presentation to the senses is the truth: hence, he observed, Homer had well sung of Hector in his swoon that he lay "with other thoughts." Democritus, then, does not use the term mind to denote a faculty conversant with truth, but regards mind as identical with soul. Anaxagoras, however, is less exact in his use of the terms. In many places he speaks of mind as the cause of goodness and order, but elsewhere he identifies it with the soul: as where he attributes it to all animals, both great and small, high and low. As a matter of fact, however, mind in the sense of intelligence would not seem to be present in all animals alike, nor even in all men.

404b

    Those, then, who have directed their attention to the motion of the animate being, conceived the soul as that which is most capable of causing motion: while those who laid stress on its knowledge and perception of all that exists identified the soul with the ultimate principles, whether they recognized a plurality of these or only one. Thus Empedocles compounded soul out of all the elements, while at the same time regarding each one of them as a soul. His words are "With earth we see earth, with water water, with air bright air, but ravaging fire by fire, love by love, and strife by gruesome strife." In the same manner Plato in the *Timaeus* constructs the soul out of the elements. Like, he there maintains, is known by like, and the things we know we composed of the ultimate principles. In like manner it was explained in the lectures on philosophy, that the self-animal or universe is made up of the idea of One, and of the idea-numbers Two, or primary length, Three, primary breadth, and Four, primary depth, and similarly with all the rest of the ideas. And again this has been put in another way as follows: reason is the One, knowledge is the Two, because it proceeds by a single road to one conclusion, opinion is the number of a surface, Three, and sensation the number of a solid, Four. In fact, according to them the numbers, though they are the ideas themselves, or the ultimate principles, are nevertheless derived from elements. And things are judged, some by reason, others by knowledge, others again by opinion and others by sensation: while these idea-numbers are forms of things. And since the soul was held to be thus cognitive as well as capable of causing motion, some thinkers have combined the two and defined the soul as a self-moving number.

But there are differences of opinion as to the nature and number of the ultimate principles, especially between those thinkers who make the principles corporeal and those who make them incorporeal; and again between both of these and others who combine the two and take their principles from both. But, further, they differ also as to

405a

their number: some assuming a single principle, some a plurality. And, when they come to give an account of the soul, they do so in strict accordance with their several views. For they have assumed, not unnaturally, that the soul is that primary cause which in its own nature is capable of producing motion. And this is why some identified soul with fire, this being the element which is made up of the finest particles and is most nearly incorporeal, while further it is preeminently an element which both moves and sets other things in motion. Democritus has expressed more neatly the reason for each of these facts. Soul he regards as identical with mind, and this he makes to consist of the primary indivisible bodies and considers it to be a cause of motion from the fineness of its particles and their shape. Now the shape which is most susceptible of motion is the spherical; and of atoms of this shape mind, like fire, consists. Anaxagoras, while apparently understanding by mind something different from soul, as we remarked above, really treats both as a single nature, except that it is preeminently mind which he takes as his first principle; he says at any rate that mind alone of things that exist is simple, unmixed, pure. But he refers both knowledge and motion to the same principle, when he says that mind sets the universe in motion. Thales, too, apparently, judging from the anecdotes related of him, conceived soul as a cause of motion, if it be true that he affirmed the lodestone to possess soul, because it attracts iron. Diogenes, however, as also some others, identified soul with air. Air, they thought, is made up of the finest particles and is the first principle: and this explains the fact that the soul knows and is a cause of motion, knowing by virtue of being the primary element from which all else is derived, and causing motion by the extreme fineness of its parts. Heraclitus takes soul for his first principle, as he identifies it with the vapor from which he derives all other things, and further says that it is the least corporeal of things and in ceaseless flux; and that it is by something in motion that what is in motion is known; for he, like most philosophers, conceived all that exists to be in motion. Alcmaeon, too, seems to have had a similar conception. For soul, he maintains, is immortal because it is like the beings which are immortal; and it has this attribute in virtue of being ever in motion: for he attributes continuous and unending motion to everything which is divine, moon, sun, stars, and the whole heaven.

405b   Among cruder thinkers there have been some, like Hippon, who have even asserted the soul to be water. The reason for this view seems to have been the fact that in all animals the seed is moist: in fact, Hippon refutes those who make the soul to be blood by pointing out that the seed is not blood, and that this seed is the rudimentary soul. Others, again, like Critias, maintain the soul to be blood, holding that it is sentience which is most distinctive of soul and that this is due to the nature of blood. Thus each of the four elements except earth has found its supporter. Earth, however, has not been put forward by anyone, except by those who have explained the soul to be derived from, or identical with, all the elements.

Thus practically all define the soul by three characteristics, motion, perception, and incorporeality; and each of these characteristics is referred to the ultimate principles. Hence all who define soul by its capacity for knowledge either make it an element or derive it from the elements, being on this point, with one exception, in general agreement. Like, they tell us, is known by like; and therefore, since the soul knows all things, they say it consists of all the ultimate principles. Thus those thinkers who admit only one cause and one element, as fire or air, assume the soul also to be one element; while those who admit a plurality of principles assume plurality also in the soul. Anaxagoras alone says that mind cannot be acted upon and has nothing in common with any other thing. How, if such be its nature, it will know anything and how its knowledge is to be explained, he has omitted to state; nor do his utterances afford a clue. All those who introduce pairs of opposites among their principles make the soul also to consist of opposites; while those who take one or other of the two opposites, either hot or cold or something else of the sort, reduce the soul also to one or other of these elements. Hence, too, they etymologize according to their theories; some identify soul with heat, deriving ζῆν [to live] from ζεῖν [to boil], and contend that this identity accounts for the word for life; others say that what is cold is called soul from the respiratory process and consequent "cooling down," deriving ψυχή [soul] from ψύχειν [to grow cold]. Such, then, are the views regarding soul which have come down to us and the grounds on which they are held.

3.   We have to consider in the first place the subject of motion. For, unless I am mistaken, the definition of soul as the self-moving, or as that which is capable of self-motion, misrepresents its essential nature: nay, more; it is quite impossible for soul to have the attribute of motion at all. To begin with, it has been already stated that a thing may cause motion without necessarily being moved itself. A thing is always moved in one of two ways; that is, either indirectly, through something else, or directly, of and through itself. We say things are moved through something else when they are in something else that is moved: as, for instance, sailors on board a ship: for they do not move in the same sense as the ship, for the ship moves of itself, they because they are in something else which is moved. This is evident if we consider the members of the body: for the motion

proper to the feet and so to men also is walking, but it is not attributable to our sailors in the case supposed. There being thus two senses in which the term "to be moved" is used, we are now inquiring whether it is of and through itself that the soul is moved and partakes of motion.

Of motion there are four species, change of place or locomotion, change of quality or alteration, diminution and augmentation. It is, then, with one or more or all of these species that the soul will move. If it is not indirectly or *per accidens* that it moves, motion will be a natural attribute of soul; and, if this be so, it will also have position in space, since all the aforesaid species of motion are in space. *But,* if it be the essential nature of soul to move itself, motion will not be an accidental attribute of soul, as it is of whiteness or the length of three cubits; for these are also moved, but *per accidens, viz.* by the motion of the body to which these attributes belong. This, too, is why these attributes have no place belonging to them; but the soul will have a place, if indeed motion is its natural attribute.

Further, if it moves naturally, then it will also move under constraint; and, if under constraint, then also naturally. So likewise with rest. For, as it remains at rest naturally in any state into which it moves naturally, so similarly it remains at rest by constraint in any state into which it moves by constraint. But what is meant by constrained motions or states of rest of the soul it is not easy to explain, even though we give free play to fancy. Again, if its motion tends upward, it will be fire; if downward, earth; these being the motions proper to these natural bodies. And the same argument applies to directions of motion which are intermediate.

Again, since it appears that the soul sets the body in motion, it may reasonably be supposed to impart to it the motion which it has itself: and, if so, then conversely it is true to say that the motion which the soul has itself is the motion which the body has. Now the motion of the body is motion in space: therefore the motion of the soul is also motion in space, whether the whole soul so move, or only the parts, the whole remaining at rest. But, 406b if this is admissible, the soul might also conceivably quit the body and re-enter; and this would involve the consequence that dead animals may rise again.

To return now to motion *per accidens,* soul might certainly thus be moved by something external as well:— for the animal might be thrust by force. But a thing which has self-motion as part of its essential nature cannot be moved from without except incidentally; any more than that which is good in itself can be means to an end, or that which is good for its own sake can be so for the sake of something else. But, supposing the soul to be moved at all, one would say that sensible things would be the most likely to move it.

Again, even if soul does move itself, this is equivalent to saying that it is moved; and, all motion being defined as displacement of the thing moved *quâ* moved, it will follow that the soul will be displaced from its own essential nature, if it be true that its self-movement is not an accident, but that motion belongs to the essence of soul in and of itself. Some say that the soul in fact moves the body, in which it is, in the same way in which it moves itself. So, for example, Democritus; and herein he resembled Philippus, the comic poet, who tells us that Daedalus endowed the wooden Aphrodite with motion, simply by pouring in quicksilver: this is very similar to what Democritus says. For according to him the spherical atoms, which from their nature can never remain still, being moved, tend to draw the whole body after them and thus set it in motion. But do these same atoms, we shall ask in our turn, produce rest, as well as motion? How this should be, it is difficult, if not impossible, to say. And, speaking generally, it is not in this way that the soul would seem to move the animal, but by means of purpose of some sort, that is, thought.

In the same way the Platonic Timaeus explains on physical grounds that the soul sets the body in motion, for by its own motion it sets the body also in motion, because it is closely interwoven with it. For when it had been made out of the elements and divided in harmonical ratios in order that it might have a native perception of proportion and that the universe might move in harmonic revolutions, he, the creator, proceeded to bend the straight line into a circle; and then to split the one circle into two, 407a intersecting at two points; and one of the two circles he split into seven, the revolutions of heaven being regarded as the motions of the soul. In the first place, it is not right to call the soul a magnitude. For by the soul of the universe Timaeus clearly intends something of the same sort as what is known as mind: he can hardly mean that it is like the sensitive or appetitive soul, whose movements are not circular. But the thinking mind is one and continuous in the same sense as the process of thinking. Now thinking consists of thoughts. But the unity of these thoughts is a unity of succession, the unity of a number, and not the unity of a magnitude. This being so, neither is mind continuous in this latter sense, but either it is without parts or else it is continuous in a different sense from an extended magnitude. For how can it possibly think if it be a magnitude? Will it think with some one or other of its parts: such parts being taken either in the sense of magnitudes or in the sense of points, if a point can be called a part? If it be with parts in the sense of points, and there is an infinity of these, clearly mind will never reach the end of them; while, if they be taken in the sense of magnitudes, mind will have the same thoughts times without end. But experience shows that we can think a thought once and no more. Again, if it be enough for the soul to apprehend with one or other of its parts, what need is there for it to be moving in a circle or to have magnitude at all? But, if it is necessary to thought that the mind should bring the whole circle into contact, what does the contact of the several parts mean? Again, how will it think that which is divisible by means of that which is without parts, or that which is without parts by means of that which is divisible? It must be mind which is meant by the circle in question. For when mind moves it thinks; when a circle moves it revolves. If, then, thought is a revolution, the circle which has such a revolution must be mind. But then it will go on thinking of something for ever, for this is required by the eternity of the revolution. To practical thinking there are limits, for it always implies an external end; while speculative thinking is determined in the same way as the logical explanations which express it. Now every explanation consists either in definition or in demonstration. But demonstrations have a premiss for starting-point and reach a kind of goal in the inference or conclusion; while, even if they never reach a conclusion, at all events they do not revert to the starting-point, but with the aid of a succession of middle terms and extremes advance in a straight line. But circular movement returns to the point from which it started. Definitions, too, are all determinate. Besides, if the same revolution recurs again and again, the mind will be obliged to think the same thing again and again. Further, it is a sort of rest or coming to a halt, and not motion, which thinking resembles: and we may say the same of the syllogism. Nor, again, will that which does not move easily, but under constraint, even realize happiness. If the motion of soul be not its essence, it will

407b be an unnatural motion. And the entanglement of the mind in the body without the possibility of release is painful; nay, it is to be avoided, if indeed it is really better for mind to be independent of body, a view commonly expressed and widely accepted. Also it is not clear why the heaven revolves in a circle; seeing that circular motion is neither implied by the essence of soul (that form of movement being indeed merely accidental to it), nor due to the body: on the contrary it is rather the soul which causes the motion of the body. Besides, we are not even told that it is better so: yet surely the reason why God made the soul revolve in a circle ought to have been that movement was better for it than rest, and this form of movement better than any other.

But such an inquiry as this belongs more appropriately to a different subject: so let us dismiss it for the present. We may, however, note here another absurdity which is involved in this as in most other theories concerning the soul. They attach the soul to, and enclose it in, body, without further determining why this happens and what is the condition of the body. And yet some such explanation would seem to be required, as it is owing to their relationship that the one acts, the other is acted upon, that the one is moved, and the other causes it to move; and between two things taken at random no such mutual relations exist. The supporters of such theories merely undertake to explain the nature of the soul. Of the body which is to receive it they have nothing more to say: just as if it were possible for any soul taken at random, according to the Pythagorean stories, to pass into any body. This is absurd, for each body appears to have a distinctive form or shape of its own. It is just like talking of a transmigration of carpentry into flutes: for the craft must employ the right tools and the soul the right body.

4. There is yet another opinion concerning soul which
has come down to us, commending itself to many minds
as readily as any that is put forward, although it has been
severely criticized even in the popular discussions of the
present day. The soul is asserted to be a kind of harmony,
for harmony is on this view a blending or combining of
opposites, and the components of the body are opposites.
And yet this harmony must mean either a certain proportion in the components or else the combining of them;
and the soul cannot possibly be either of these. Furthermore,
to cause motion is no attribute of a harmony: yet this
function more than any other is all but universally assigned   408a
to soul. Again, it is more in harmony with the facts to
apply the term harmony to health or bodily excellence
generally than to soul, as is very clearly seen when we
try to assign to a harmony of whatever kind the affections
or functions of the soul: it is difficult to harmonize them.

Further, if we use the word harmony with a twofold
application; first, and in its most natural sense, of those
magnitudes which have motion and position, to denote
the combining of them into a whole, when they are so
closely fitted together that they do not admit between them
anything of the same kind; and then in a secondary sense
to denote the proportion subsisting between the components
of a mixture: in neither sense is it reasonable to call soul
a harmony. The view which regards it as a combining of
the parts of the body is singularly open to criticism. For
there are many combinings of the parts, and they combine
in many ways. What part, then, is that whose combining
with the rest we must assume to be the intellect, and in
what way does it combine? Or again, what of the sensitive
and appetitive faculties? But it is equally absurd to regard
the soul as the proportion determining the mixture. For
the elements are not mixed in the same proportion in flesh

as in bone. Thus it will follow that there are many souls, and that, too, all over the body, if we assume that all members consist of the elements variously commingled and that the proportion determining the mixture is a harmony, that is, soul. This is a question we might ask Empedocles; who says that each of the parts is determined by a certain proportion. Is the soul, then, this proportion, or is it rather developed in the frame as something distinct? And, further, is it a mixture at random or a mixture in the right proportion which he ascribes to Love: and, if the latter, is Love the proportion itself or something other than the proportion and distinct from it? Such, then, are the difficulties involved in this view. On the other hand, if soul is something distinct from the mixture, how comes it that it is destroyed simultaneously with the disappearance of the quiddity of the flesh and of the other parts of the animal? And, further, assuming that each of the separate parts has not a soul of its own unless the soul be the proportion of their admixture, what is it that perishes when the soul quits the body?

From what has been said it is clear that the soul cannot be a harmony and cannot revolve in a circle. But incidentally it can, as we have seen, move and set itself in motion: for instance, the body in which it is may move, and be set in motion by the soul: otherwise it cannot possibly move from place to place. The question whether the soul is moved would more naturally arise in view of such facts as the following. The soul is said to feel pain and joy, confidence and fear, and again to be angry, to perceive and to think; and all these states are held to be movements: which might lead one to infer that soul itself is moved. But this is no necessary inference. For suppose it ever so true that to feel pain or joy and to think are movements, that to experience each of these is to be moved and that the movement

408b

is due to the soul: suppose that to be angry, for instance, or to be afraid means a particular movement of the heart, and that to think means a movement of this or of some other part, some of these movements being movements of locomotion, others of qualitative change (of what sort and how produced does not concern us here): yet, even then, to speak of the soul as feeling anger is as if one should say that the soul weaves or builds. Doubtless it would be better not to say that the soul pities or learns or thinks, but that the man does so with the soul: and this, too, not in the sense that the motion occurs in the soul, but in the sense that motion sometimes reaches to, sometimes starts from, the soul. Thus, sensation originates in particular objects, while recollection, starting from the soul, is directed towards the movements or traces of movements in the sense-organs. But intellect would seem to be developed in us as a self-existing substance and to be imperishable. For, if anything could destroy it, it would be the feebleness of age. But, as things are, no doubt what occurs is the same as in the case of the sense-organs. If an aged man could procure an eye of the right sort, he would see just as well as a young man. Hence old age must be due to an affection or state not of the soul as such, but of that in which the soul resides, just as is the case in intoxication and disease. In like manner, then, thought and the exercise of knowledge are enfeebled through the loss of something else within, but are in themselves impassive. But reasoning, love, and hatred are not attributes of the thinking faculty but of its individual possessor, in so far as he possesses it. Hence when this possessor perishes, there is neither memory nor love: for these never did belong to the thinking faculty, but to the composite whole which has perished, while the intellect is doubtless a thing more divine and is impassive.

From the foregoing it is clear that the soul is incapable of motion; and, if it is not moved at all, clearly it does not move itself. Now of all the views that have been put forward by far the most irrational is that which makes the soul a self-moving number. Its supporters are involved in many impossibilities, not only in those which arise from attributing motion to the soul, but also in others of a special character due to calling it a number. For how are we to

409a conceive of a unit, a thing which is without parts or differences, as in motion? By what would it be moved, and in what way? For if it is capable of imparting motion as well as of being moved, it must admit differences. Further, since they say that a line by its motion generates a surface and that a point by its motion generates a line, the movements of the units will also be lines, for a point is a unit having position. But the number of the soul must, from the nature of the case, be somewhere and have position. Again, if you subtract a number or unit from a number, a different number remains: whereas plants and many animals continue to live when divided and seem to have specifically the same soul in each segment. Besides, it would seem to make no difference whether we say units or tiny particles. For if the little round atoms of Democritus be converted into points and only their sum-total be retained, in such sum-total there will still be a part which moves and a part which is moved, just as there is in that which is extended. The truth of this statement does not depend upon the size of the atoms, whether great or small, but upon the fact that there is a sum-total or quantity of them. Hence there must be something to set the units in motion. But if in the animal the part which causes motion is the soul, then it is so likewise in the number: so that it will not be both that which causes motion and that which is moved which is the soul, but that which causes motion only. How then can this cause of motion be a unit? For if it were so there must be some difference between it and the other units. But what is there to differentiate points which are units, except position? If, then, the units, that is the points, in the body are distinct from the units of soul, the units of soul will be in the same place as the points, for each unit will occupy the space of a point. And yet if two things can be in the same place, why not an infinite number? When the place which things occupy is indivisible, the things themselves are also indivisible. If, on the other hand, the number of the soul consists of the points in the body, or if the soul is the number of such points, why are not all bodies possessed of soul? For in all bodies there would seem to be points: nay, an infinity of points. And, further, how can the points be separated and set free from the bodies to which they belong; unless, indeed, we are prepared to resolve lines into points?

5.   It comes to this, then, as we have said, first, that this view coincides with that which makes of the soul a body composed of fine particles; next, that its agreement with Democritus as to the manner in which he makes the body to be moved by the soul gives it an especial absurdity of   409b
its own. If the soul resides in the whole sentient body, on the assumption that the soul is a sort of body it necessarily follows that two bodies occupy the same space. Those who call the soul a number have to assume many points in the one point, or else that everything corporeal has a soul; unless the number that comes to exist in the body is a different number, quite distinct from the sum of the points already present in the body. Hence it follows that the animal is moved by the number in the same way precisely as we said Democritus moved it. For what difference does it make whether we speak of small round atoms or large units,

or indeed of units in spatial motion at all? Either way it is necessary to make the motion of the animal depend on the motion of these atoms or units. Such, then, are some of the difficulties confronting those who join motion and number: and there are many others, since it is impossible that the conjunction of motion with number should form even an attribute, much less the definition, of soul. This will be evident if we try to deduce from this definition the affections and functions of the soul; its reasonings, perceptions, pleasures, pains, and so forth. For, as we said above, from the account given it is difficult even to divine what these functions are.

Three modes of defining the soul have come down to us: some defined it as that which, in virtue of its self-motion, is most capable of causing motion; others as the body which consists of the finest particles, or which is more nearly incorporeal than anything else. And we have pretty fully explained what difficulties and inconsistencies these views present. It remains to consider what is meant by saying that the soul is composed of the elements. Soul, we are told, is composed of the elements in order that it may perceive and know each several thing. But this theory necessarily involves many impossibilities. For it is assumed that like is known by like; which implies that soul is identical with the things that it knows. These elements, however, are not all that exists: there are a great, or perhaps we should say rather, an infinite number of other things as well, namely, those which are compounded of the elements. Granted, then, that it is possible for the soul to know and to perceive the constituent elements of all these composite things, with what will it know or perceive the compound itself? I mean, what God or man is; what flesh or bone is: and so likewise with regard to any other composite thing.

410a   For it is not elements taken anyhow which constitute this or that thing, but only those which are united in a given proportion or combination, as Empedocles says of bone:

> Then did the bounteous earth in broad-bosomed crucibles win out of eight parts two from the sheen of moisture and four from the fire-god; and the bones came into being all white.

It is therefore of no use for the elements to be in the soul, unless it also contains their proportions and the mode of combining them. For each element will know its like, but there will be nothing to know bone or man, unless these also are to be present in the soul: which, I need hardly say, is impossible. Who would ask if stone or man resides in the soul? And similarly with that which is good and that which is not good: and so for all the rest.

Being, again, is a term which has various meanings, signifying sometimes the particular thing, sometimes quantity or quality or any other of the categories which have been already determined. Is the soul to be derived from all of these, or not? It cannot be: the general opinion is that there are no elements common to all the categories. Does the soul, then, consist of those elements alone which are the elements of substances? How then does it know each of the other categories? Or will they say that each summum genus has special elements and principles of its own, and that the soul is composed of these? Then soul will be at once quantity, quality, and substance. But it is impossible from the elements of quantity to derive substance or anything but quantity. These, then, and others like them are the difficulties which confront those who derive soul from all the elements. There is a further inconsistency in maintaining that like is unaffected by like and yet at the same time that like perceives like and knows like by like. But they assume that perceiving is a sort of being acted upon or moved. And the same holds of thinking and knowing.

Of the many problems and difficulties involved in holding with Empedocles that each thing is known through corporeal elements and by reference to its like [*what has just been said is evidence*].—For, it would seem, whatever within the bodies of animals consists entirely of earth, such as bones, sinews, hair, perceives nothing at all, and con-
410b sequently cannot perceive its like; as in consistency it should. Moreover, each one of the elemental principles will have a far larger share of ignorance than of intelligence; there being many things of which it will be ignorant and only one which it will know: in fact, it will be ignorant of all besides that one. It follows, for Empedocles at any rate, that God is quite the most unintelligent of beings. There is one of the elements, viz. Strife, which he, and he alone, will not know, while mortal things, being composed of all the elements, will know them all. And in general, seeing that everything is either an element or derived from one or more or all elements, why should not all things that exist have soul? For they must certainly know one thing or some things or all. It must further be asked what it is that gives them unity. For the elements, at all events, correspond to matter. That other principle, whatever it be, which holds them together, is supreme. Yet it is impossible that anything should be superior to the soul and overrule it; and still more impossible that anything should overrule intelligence. This, it may reasonably be held, has a natural priority and authority. Yet we are told that the elements are prior to all other things that exist.

And it is characteristic, alike of those who derive the soul from the elements on the ground of perception and knowledge, and of those who define it as the thing most capable of causing motion, that their assertions do not apply to soul in every form. For not all sentient beings can cause motion; some animals are seen to be stationary in one place. And yet it is at all events a received view that this, namely, change of place, is the one form of motion which the soul imparts to the animal. Similarly with those who derive intelligence and the faculty of sense from the elements. For plants are found to live without any share in locomotion or sensation, and many animals to be destitute of thought. If we waive this point and assume intellect to be a part of the soul, and the faculty of sense likewise, even then their statements would not apply generally to all soul, nor to the whole of any one soul. The account given in the so-called Orphic poems is open to the same strictures. For the soul, it is there asserted, enters from the universe in the process of respiration, being borne upon the winds. Now it is impossible that this should be so with plants or even with some animals, seeing that they do not all respire: a point which the upholders of this theory have overlooked. And if the soul is to be constructed out of the elements, there is no need to employ them all, the one of a pair of contraries being sufficient to discern both itself and its opposite. For by that which is straight we discern both the straight and the crooked, the carpenter's rule being the test of both. On the other hand that which is crooked is not a test of itself or of that which is straight.

411a

There are some, too, who say that soul is interfused throughout the universe: which is perhaps why Thales supposed all things to be full of gods. But his view presents some difficulties. For why should the soul not produce an animal, when present in air or fire, and yet do so when present in the compounds of these elements: and that, too, though in the former case it is believed to be purer? One might also inquire why the soul present in air is purer and more immortal than soul in animals. Whichever of the two suppositions open to us we adopt is absurd and irrational. To speak of fire or air as an animal is very irrational; and on the other hand not to call them animals, if they contain soul, is absurd. But it would seem that the reason why they suppose soul to be in these elements is that the whole is homogeneous with its parts. So that they cannot help regarding universal soul as also homogeneous with the parts of it in animals, since it is through something of the surrounding element being cut off and enclosed in animals that the animals become endowed with soul. But if the air when split up remains homogeneous, and yet soul is divisible into non-homogeneous parts, it is clear that, although one part of soul may be present in the air, there is another part which is not. Either, then, soul must be homogeneous, or else it cannot be present in every part of the universe.

From what has been said it is evident that it is not because the soul is compounded of the elements that knowledge belongs to it, nor is it correct or true to say that the soul is moved. Knowledge, however, is an attribute of the soul, and so are perception, opinion, desire, wish, and appetency generally; animal locomotion also is pro-
411b   duced by the soul; and likewise growth, maturity, and decay. Shall we then say that each of these belongs to the whole soul, that we think, that is, and perceive and are moved and in each of the other operations act and are acted upon with the whole soul, or that the different operations are to be assigned to different parts? And what of life itself? Does it reside in any single one or more or all of these parts? Or has it a cause entirely distinct? Now some say that the soul is divisible and that one part of it thinks, another desires. What is it then which holds the soul together, if naturally divisible? Assuredly it is not the body: on the contrary, the soul seems rather to hold the body

together; at all events, when it has departed, the body disperses in air and rots away. If, then, the unity of soul is due to some other thing, that other thing would be, properly speaking, soul. We shall need, then, to repeat the inquiry respecting it also, whether it is one or manifold. For, if it has unity, why not attribute unity to the soul itself at the outset? If, however, it be divisible, then again reason will go on to ask what it is that holds it together, and so the inquiry will go on to infinity. It might also be asked what power each of the parts of the soul exercises in the body. For, if the entire soul holds together the whole body, then each of its parts ought properly to hold together some part of the body. But this seems impossible. For it is difficult even to conjecture what part the intellect will hold together or how it can hold any part together. It is found that plants, and among animals certain insects or annelida, live when divided, which implies that the soul in their segments is specifically, though not numerically, the same. At any rate, each of the two segments retains sentience and the power of locomotion for some time: that they do not continue to do so is not surprising, as they lack the organs requisite to maintain their nature. But none the less all the parts of the soul are contained in each of the two segments, and the two halves of the soul are homogeneous alike with one another and with the whole; a fact which implies that, while the parts of the soul are inseparable from one another, the soul as a whole is divisible. It would seem that the vital principle in plants also is a sort of soul. For this principle is the only one common to plants and animals; and, while it can be separated from the sensitive principle, no being which has sensation is without it.

BOOK II

1.   So much for the theories of soul handed down by   412a
our predecessors. Let us, then, make a fresh start and try
to determine what soul is and what will be its most com-
prehensive definition. Now there is one class of existent
things which we call substance, including under the term,
firstly, matter, which in itself is not this or that; secondly,
shape or form, in virtue of which the term this or that
is at once applied; thirdly, the whole made up of matter
and form. Matter is identical with potentiality, form with
actuality. And there are two meanings of actuality: knowledge illustrates the one, exercise of knowledge the other.
Now bodies above all things are held to be substances,
particularly such bodies as are the work of nature; for to
these all the rest owe their origin. Of natural bodies some
possess life and some do not: where by life we mean the
power of self-nourishment and of independent growth and
decay. Consequently every natural body possessed of life
must be substance, and substance of the composite order.

37

And since in fact we have here body with a certain attribute, namely, the possession of life, the body will not be the soul: for the body is not an attribute of a subject, it stands rather for a subject of attributes, that is, matter. It must follow, then, that soul is substance in the sense that it is the form of a natural body having in it the capacity of life. Such substance is actuality. The soul, therefore, is the actuality of the body above described. But the term 'actuality' is used in two senses; in the one it answers to knowledge, in the other to the exercise of knowledge. Clearly in this case it is analogous to knowledge: for sleep, as well as waking, implies the presence of soul; and, whilst waking is analogous to the exercise of knowledge, sleep is analogous to the possession of knowledge without its exercise; and in the same individual the possession of knowledge comes in order of time before its exercise. Hence soul is the first

412b   actuality of a natural body having in it the capacity of life. And a body which is possessed of organs answers to this description.—We may note that the parts of plants, as well as those of animals, are organs, though of a very simple sort: for instance, a leaf is the sheath of the pod and the pod of the fruit. The roots, again, are analogous to the mouths of animals, both serving to take in nourishment.—If, then, we have to make a general statement touching soul in all its forms, the soul will be the first actuality of a natural body furnished with organs. Hence there is no need to inquire whether soul and body are one, any more than whether the wax and the imprint are one; or, in general, whether the matter of a thing is the same with that of which it is the matter. For, of all the various meanings borne by the terms unity and being, actuality is the meaning which belongs to them by the fullest right.

It has now been stated in general terms what soul

is, namely, substance as notion or form. And this is the quiddity of such and such a body. Suppose, for example, that any instrument, say, an axe, were a natural body, its axeity would be its substance, would in fact be its soul. If this were taken away, it would cease, except in an equivocal sense, to be an axe. But the axe is after all an axe. For it is not of a body of this kind that the soul is the quiddity, that is, the notion or form, but of a natural body of a particular sort, having in itself the origination of motion and rest.

Further, we must view our statement in the light of the parts of the body. For, if the eye were an animal, eyesight would be its soul, this being the substance as notion or form of the eye. The eye is the matter of eyesight, and in default of eyesight it is no longer an eye, except equivocally, like an eye in stone or in a picture. What has been said of the part must be understood to apply to the whole living body; for, as the sensation of a part of the body is to that part, so is sensation as a whole to the whole sentient body as such. By that which has in it the capacity of life is meant not the body which has lost its soul, but that which possesses it. Now the seed in animals, like the fruit in plants, is that which is potentially such and such a body. As, then, the cutting of the axe or the seeing of the eye is full actuality, so, too, is the waking state; while the soul is actuality in the same sense as eyesight and the capacity of the instrument. The body, on the other hand, is simply that which is potentially existent. But, just as in the one case the eye means the pupil in conjunction with the eyesight, so in the other soul and body together 413a constitute the animal.

Now it needs no proof that the soul—or if it is divisible into parts, certain of its parts—cannot be separated from the body, for there are cases where the actuality belongs to the parts themselves. There is, however, no reason why some parts should not be separated, if they are not the actualities of any body whatever. Again, it is not clear whether the soul may not be the actuality of the body as the sailor is of the ship. This, then, may suffice for an outline or provisional sketch of soul.

2. But, as it is from the things which are naturally obscure, though more easily recognized by us, that we proceed to what is clear and, in the order of thought, more knowable, we must employ this method in trying to give a fresh account of soul. For it is not enough that the defining statement should set forth the fact, as most definitions do; it should also contain and present the cause: whereas in practice what is stated in the definition is usually no more than a conclusion. For example, what is quadrature? The construction of an equilateral rectangle equal in area to a given oblong. But such a definition expresses merely the conclusion. Whereas, if you say that quadrature is the discovery of a mean proportional, then you state the reason.

We take, then, as our starting-point for discussion that it is life which distinguishes the animate from the inanimate. But the term life is used in various senses; and, if life is present in but a single one of these senses, we speak of a thing as living. Thus there is intellect, sensation, motion from place to place and rest, the motion concerned with nutrition and, further, decay and growth. Hence it is that all plants are supposed to have life. For apparently they have within themselves a faculty and principle whereby they grow and decay in opposite directions. For plants do not grow upwards without growing downwards; they grow in both directions equally, in fact in all directions, as many as are constantly nourished and therefore continue to live, so long as they are capable of absorbing nutriment. This

form of life can be separated from the others, though in
mortal creatures the others cannot be separated from it.
In the case of plants the fact is manifest: for they have
no other faculty of soul at all.

It is, then, in virtue of this principle that all living   413b
things live, whether animals or plants. But it is sensation
primarily which constitutes the animal. For, provided they
have sensation, even those creatures which are devoid of
movement and do not change their place are called animals
and are not merely said to be alive. Now the primary sense
in all animals is touch. But, as the nutritive faculty may
exist without touch or any form of sensation, so also touch
may exist apart from the other senses. By nutritive faculty
we mean the part of the soul in which even plants share.
Animals, however, are found universally to have the sense
of touch: why this is so in each of the two cases will be
stated hereafter.

For the present it may suffice to say that the soul
is the origin of the functions above enumerated and is
determined by them, namely, by capacities of nutrition,
sensation, thought, and by motion. But whether each one
of these is a soul or part of a soul and, if a part, whether
it is only logically distinct or separable in space also is
a question, the answer to which is in some cases not hard
to see: other cases present difficulties. For, just as in the
case of plants some of them are found to live when divided
and separated from each other (which implies that the soul
in each plant, though actually one, is potentially several
souls), so, too, when insects or annelida are cut up, we
see the same thing happen with other varieties of soul:
I mean, each of the segments has sensation and moves
from place to place, and, if it has sensation, it has also
imagination and appetency. For, where there is sensation,
there is also pleasure and pain: and, where these are, desire

also must of necessity be present. But as regards intellect and the speculative faculty the case is not yet clear. It would seem, however, to be a distinct species of soul, and it alone is capable of separation from the body, as that which is eternal from that which is perishable. The remaining parts of the soul are, as the foregoing consideration shows, not separable in the way that some allege them to be: at the same time it is clear that they are logically distinct. For the faculties of sensation and of opinion taken in the abstract are distinct, since to have sensation and to opine are distinct. And so it is likewise with each of the other faculties above mentioned. Again, while some animals possess all these functions, others have only some of them, others only one. It is this which will differentiate animal from animal. The reason why this is so must be investigated hereafter. The case is similar with the several senses: some animals have all of them, others some of them, others again only one, the most indispensable, that is, touch.

414a

Now "that by which we live and have sensation" is a phrase with two meanings, answering to the two meanings of "that by which we know" (the latter phrase means, firstly, knowledge and, secondly, soul, by either of which we say we know). Similarly that by which we have health means either health itself or a certain part, if not the whole, of the body. Now of these knowledge and health are the shape and in some sort form, the notion and virtual activity, of that which is capable of receiving in the one case knowledge, in the other health: that is to say, it is in that which is acted upon or conditioned that the activity of the causal agencies would seem to take effect. Now the soul is that whereby primarily we live, perceive, and have understanding: therefore it will be a species of notion or form, not matter or substratum. Of the three meanings of substance mentioned above, form, matter, and the whole made up of these two, matter is potentiality and form is actuality. And, since the whole made up of the two is endowed with soul, the body is not the actuality of soul, but soul the actuality of a particular body. Hence those are right who regard the soul as not independent of body and yet at the same time as not itself a species of body. It is not body, but something belonging to body, and therefore resides in body and, what is more, in such and such a body. Our predecessors were wrong in endeavoring to fit the soul into a body without further determination of the nature and qualities of that body: although we do not even find that of any two things taken at random the one will admit the other. And this result is what we might expect. For the actuality of each thing comes naturally to be developed in the potentiality of each thing: in other words, in the appropriate matter. From these considerations, then, it is manifest that soul is a certain actuality, a notion or form, of that which has the capacity to be endowed with soul.

3.　Of the powers of soul above mentioned, namely, those of nutrition, appetency, sensation, locomotion, and understanding, some living things, as we remarked, possess all, others some, others again only one. Plants possess the nutritive faculty only: other things along with this have sensation; and, if sensation, then also appetency: where under appetency we include desire, anger, and wish. But all animals have at least one sense, touch: and, where sensation is found, there is pleasure and pain; and, where these are, there also is desire, desire being appetite for what is pleasurable. Again, they have a sensation concerned with nutriment, touch being such a sense. For it is by what is dry and moist, hot and cold, that all living things are nourished (and these qualities are perceived by touch, whereas the other sensibles are not,

414b

except incidentally): for sound, color, and odor contribute
nothing to nutriment, while flavor is one of the tangible
objects. Hunger again, and thirst are forms of desire, the
one for what is hot or dry, the other for what is cold
or moist. Flavor is, as it were, the seasoning of these. We
will deal with these in detail hereafter: at present let it suffice
to say that all animals which have the sense of touch are
also endowed with appetency. Whether they have imagination is not clear: this, too, must be considered later. Some
have in addition the power of locomotion. Others—that
is to say, man and any other species like man or, possibly,
superior to him—have also the thinking faculty and intellect.

From this it is clear that there is one definition of
soul exactly as there is one definition of figure: for there
is in the one case no figure excepting triangle, quadrilateral,
and the rest, nor is there in the other any species of soul
apart from those above mentioned. Again, a definition
might be constructed which should apply to all figures,
but not specially to any species of figure. And similarly
with the species of soul above enumerated. Hence it would
be absurd here as elsewhere to seek a general definition
which will not be properly a definition of anything in existence and will not be applicable to the particular irreducible
species before us, to the neglect of the definition which
is so applicable.

The types of soul resemble the series of figures. For,
alike in figures and in things animate, the earlier form exists
potentially in the later, as, for instance, the triangle potentially in the quadrilateral, and the nutritive faculty in
that which has sensation. So that we must examine in each
case separately, what is the soul of plant, of man, or of
beast. Why they are related in this order of succession remains to be considered. There is no sensitive faculty apart
from the nutritive: and yet the latter exists without the

former in plants. Again, none of the other senses is found   415a
apart from touch; while touch is found apart from the
others, many animals having neither sight nor hearing nor
sense of smell. Also of these which possess sensation, some
can move from place to place, others cannot. Lastly and
most rarely, they have the reasoning faculty and thought.
For those perishable creatures which possess reason are
endowed with all the other species of soul, but not all those
which possess each of the other faculties have reason.
Indeed, some of them have not even imagination, while
others live by imagination alone. As for the speculative
intellect, it calls for a separate discussion. Meanwhile it
is clear that an account of the several faculties is at the
same time the most appropriate account of soul.

4. The inquirer who approaches this subject must ascertain what each of these faculties is before he proceeds to
investigate the questions next in order and so forth. But
if we are asked to state what each of these is; that is to
say, what the cognitive, sensitive, and nutritive faculties
respectively are, we must begin by stating what the act
of thinking is and what the act of sensation is. For activities
and functions are logically prior to faculties. But, if so,
and if a study of the correlative objects should have pre-
ceded, these objects will for the same reason have to be
defined first: I mean, nutriment and the sensible and intelligible. Consequently we have first to treat of nutriment
and of generation.

    The nutritive soul belongs to other living things as well
as man, being the first and most widely distributed faculty,
in virtue of which all things possess life. Its functions are
reproduction and assimilation of nutriment. For it is the
most natural function in all living things, if perfect and not
defective or spontaneously generated, to reproduce their

415b species; animal producing animal and plant plant, in order
that they may, so far as they can, share in the eternal and
the divine. For it is that which all things yearn after, and
that is the final cause of all their natural activity. Here final
cause is an ambiguous term, which denotes either the purpose
for which, or the person for whom, a thing is done. Since,
then, individual things are incapable of sharing continuously
in the eternal and the divine, because nothing in the world
of perishables can abide numerically one and the same, they
partake in the eternal and divine, each in the only way
it can, some more, some less. That is to say, each persists,
though not in itself, yet in a representative which is specifically, not numerically, one with it.

Now the soul is cause and origin of the living body.
But cause and origin are terms used in various senses:
accordingly soul is cause in the three senses of the word
already determined. For the soul is the cause of animate
bodies as being in itself the origin of motion, as final cause
and as substance. Clearly it is so as substance, substance
being the cause of all existence. And for living things
existence means life, and it is the soul which is the cause
and origin of life. Furthermore, actuality is the notion or
form of that which has potential existence. Manifestly, too,
the soul is final cause. For nature, like intelligence, acts
for a purpose, and this purpose is for it an end. Such
an end the soul is in animals, and this in the order of
nature, for all the natural bodies are instruments of soul:
and this is as true of the bodies of plants as of those of
animals, showing that all are means to the soul as end;
where end has two senses, the purposes for which and the
person for whom. Moreover, the soul is also the origin
of motion from place to place, but not all living things
have this power of locomotion. Qualitative change, also,
and growth are due to soul. For sensation is supposed

to be a sort of qualitative change, and nothing devoid of soul has sensation. The same holds of growth and decay. For nothing undergoes natural decay or growth except it be nourished, and nothing is nourished unless it shares in life. Empedocles is mistaken in adding that in plants, in so far as they strike their roots downwards, growth takes place because the earth in them has a natural tendency in this direction and that, when they shoot upwards, it is because the fire in them has a similar tendency upwards.   416a He is wrong in his view of up and down. For up and down are not the same for all individuals as for the universe. On the contrary, the roots of plants correspond to the heads of animals, if we are to make identity and diversity of organs depend upon their functions. Besides, what is it that holds together the fire and the earth, tending, as they do, in opposite directions? For they will be rent asunder, unless there is something to prevent it: while, if there is, it is this which is the soul and the cause of growth and nourishment.

Some hold the nature of fire to be singly and solely the cause of nourishment and growth. For it would seem that fire is the only body or element which of itself is nourished and grows. Hence fire might be supposed to be the operative cause, both in plants and animals. Whereas, though it is in a sense a joint cause, it is not a cause absolutely: it is rather the soul which is so. For fire goes on growing to infinity, as long as there is fuel to be consumed, but in natural wholes there is always a limit or proportion which determines growth and size. But this belongs to the soul and not to fire, to form rather than to matter.

The nutritive faculty of the soul being the same as the reproductive, it is necessary first to give a definition of nutriment. For it is by the nutritive function that this

faculty is separated off from the others. The common view
is that contrary is nutriment to contrary; though not in
every case, but wherever each of two contraries is not only
generated by, but derives growth from, the other. For many
things are derived from one another, but not all of them
are quantities: thus the sick man becomes well. But it is
found that even the contraries supposed to derive growth
from each other are not fed by one another in the same
way: while water serves to feed fire, fire is not nutriment
to water. It would seem, then, that it is in the simple bodies
above all that of two contraries one is nutriment and the
other is nourished. Yet here is a difficulty. It is said by
the one side that like is nourished by, as well as derives
its growth from, like; while the others, again, as we explained, hold that contrary is nourished by contrary, on
the ground that like cannot be affected by like, while food
undergoes change and is digested. Now change is always
in the direction of the opposite, or of the intermediate state.
Further, nutriment is acted upon by that which it nourishes,
416b   and not the latter by the former: just as the carpenter is
not affected by his material, but on the contrary the material
by the carpenter. The carpenter merely passes to activity
from inaction. But it makes a difference whether by nutriment we mean the final, or the primary, form of what
is added. If both are nutriment, the one as undigested,
the other as digested, it will be possible to use the term
nutriment in conformity with both theories. For, in so far
as it is undigested, contrary is nourished by contrary: and,
in so far as it is digested, like by like. So that clearly both
sides are in a manner partly right and partly wrong. But,
since nothing is nourished unless it possesses life, that which
is nourished must be the animate body as such: so that
nutriment also is relative to the animate being which it
nourishes: and this not incidentally merely.

There is, however, a difference between nutritivity and conducivity to growth. In so far as the animate thing is quantitative, what is taken promotes growth; in so far as it is a definite individual, what is taken nourishes. For the animate thing preserves its substance or essential nature and exists as long as it is nourished: and it causes the production, not of that which is nourished, but of another individual like it. Its essential nature already exists, and nothing generates itself, it only maintains its existence. Hence the above described principle of the soul is the power to preserve in existence that which possesses it in so far as it is a definite individual, while nutrition prepares it for activity. Therefore it cannot live when deprived of nutriment. There are, then, these three things, that which is nourished, that with which it is nourished, and that which nourishes it. The last of the three is the primary soul, that which is nourished is the body which contains the soul, that wherewith it is nourished is nutriment. As, however, it is right to name all things from the end they subserve, and the end here is reproduction of the species, the primary soul is that which is capable of reproducing the species. That with which the living thing is nourished may be understood in two senses, just as that with which one steers may mean the hand or the rudder; the former, the hand, both causing motion and being moved, the latter, the rudder, being simply moved. Now it is necessary that all food should be capable of digestion, and digestion is promoted by heat; this explains why every animate thing has warmth. This, then, is an outline of what nutriment is. It must be more clearly defined hereafter in the discussion devoted specially to it.

5.   Now that these points have been determined, let us proceed to a general discussion of all sensation. As above

remarked, sensation consists in being moved and acted upon, for it is held to be a species of qualitative change. Some add that like is in fact acted upon by like. How far this is possible or impossible we have explained in the general discussion of action and passivity. The question arises why there is no sensation of the senses themselves: that is, why they produce no sensation apart from external sensibles, though the senses contain fire, earth, and other elements, which are the objects of sensation either in themselves or through their attributes. Evidently it follows that the faculty of sensible perception exists not in activity, but only in potentiality. Hence it must be here as with the fuel which does not burn of and in itself without something to make it burn; otherwise it would kindle itself and would have no need of the fire which is actually existent. Now to have sensation has two meanings: we use the terms hearing and seeing of that which has the capacity to hear and see, even though it be at the time asleep, just as we do of that which already actually hears and sees. And therefore sensation, too, will have two meanings: it may mean either potential or actual sensation. Similarly with having sensation, whether potential or actual.

417a

Let us then first proceed on the assumption that to be acted upon or moved is identical with active operation. For movement is in fact active operation of some sort, though incomplete, as we have elsewhere explained. But in every case things are acted upon and moved by an agent in actual operation. It follows that in one sense what is acted upon is acted upon by what is like it, in another sense by what is unlike it, as we have explained. That is to say, while being acted upon it is unlike, after it has been acted upon it is like the agent.

We must also draw a distinction in regard to the terms potentiality and actuality: at present we are using them without qualification. For instance, we may use the term wise, firstly, in the sense in which we might speak of man as wise, because man is one of the genus of beings which are wise and have wisdom; secondly, in the sense in which we at once call the man wise who has learned, say, grammar. Now of these two men each possesses the capacity, but in a different sense: the one because the genus to which he belongs, that is to say, his matter, is potentially wise; the other because he is capable, if he chose, of applying the wisdom he has acquired, provided there is nothing external to hinder. Whereas he who is at the moment exercising his wisdom is in actuality and is wise in the proper sense of the term: for example, he knows the A before him. Thus the first two are both potentially wise: the first becomes wise actually after he has undergone qualitative change through instruction and often after transition from the reverse condition; while in the latter case it is by another kind of transition that the man passes from the mere possession, without the use, of sensation or grammar to the use of it.

To suffer or be acted upon, too, is a term of more than one meaning. Sometimes it means a sort of destruction by the contrary, sometimes it is rather a preservation of what is potentially existent by what is actually existent and like it, so far as likeness holds of potentiality when compared with actuality. For it is by exercise of knowledge that the possessor of knowledge becomes such in actuality: and this either is no qualitative change (for the thing develops into its own nature and actuality), or else is qualitative change of a different sort. Hence it is not right to say that that which thinks undergoes change when it thinks, any more than that the builder undergoes change when he builds. That, then, which works the change from potential existence to actuality in a thinking and intelligent being should prop-

417b

erly receive a different name and not be called instruction: while that which learns and is brought from potential to actual knowledge by that which is in actuality and capable of instructing should either not be said to suffer or be acted upon at all, or else two modes of change should be assumed, one to the negative states and the other to the normal habits and the true nature.

In the sensitive subject the first change is due to the parent: once generated it possesses sensation exactly in the same sense as we possess knowledge. And to have actual sensation corresponds to exercise of knowledge. There is this difference, however, that in the one case the causes of the activity are external: as, for instance, the objects of sight, hearing, and the other senses. The reason is that actual sensation is always of particulars, while knowledge is of universals: and these universals are, in a manner, in the soul itself. Hence it is in our power to think whenever we please, but sensation is not in our power: for the presence of the sensible object is necessary. It is much the same with the sciences which deal with sensible objects; and for the same reason, namely, that sensibles are particulars and are external.

But we shall have a further opportunity of making this clear hereafter. For the present let us be content to have established that of the two meanings of potentiality, the one according to which a child might be called potentially a general, and the other according to which a man of full age might be so called, it is the latter which applies to the faculty of sense-perception. But as this distinction has no word to make it, although the fact and the nature of the distinction have been established, we are compelled to use the terms to suffer or be acted upon and to be qualitatively changed as if they were the proper terms. Now, as has been explained, the sensitive faculty is potentially

418a

such as the sensible object is in actuality. While it is being acted upon, it is not yet similar, but, when once it has been acted upon, it is assimilated and has the same character as the sensible object.

6. In considering each separate sense we must first treat of their objects. By the sensible object may be meant any one of three things, two of which we say are perceived in themselves or directly, while the third is perceived *per accidens* or indirectly. Of the first two the one is the special object of a particular sense, the other an object common to all the senses. By a special object of a particular sense I mean that which cannot be perceived by any other sense and in respect to which deception is impossible; for example, sight is of color, hearing of sound, and taste of flavor, while touch no doubt has for its object several varieties. But at any rate each single sense judges of its proper objects and is not deceived as to the fact that there is a color or a sound; though as to what or where the colored object is or what or where the object is which produces the sound, mistake is possible. Such then, are the special objects of the several senses. By common sensibles are meant motion, rest, number, figure, size: for such qualities are not the special objects of any single sense, but are common to all. For example, a particular motion can be perceived by touch as well as by sight. What is meant by the indirect object of sense may be illustrated if we suppose that the white thing before you is Daries' son. You perceive Diares' son, but indirectly, for that which you perceive is accessory to the whiteness. Hence you are not affected by the indirect sensible as such. Of the two classes of sensibles directly perceived it is the objects special to the different senses which are properly perceptible: and it is to these that the essential character of each sense is naturally adapted.

7. The object, then, of sight is the visible: what is visible is color and something besides which can be described, though it has no name. What we mean will best be made clear as we proceed. The visible, then, is color. Now color is that with which what is visible in itself is overlaid: and, when I say in itself, I do not mean what is visible by its essence or form, but what is visible because it contains within itself the cause of visibility, namely, color. But color is universally capable of exciting change in the actually transparent, that is, in light; this being, in fact, the true nature of color. Hence color is not visible without light, but the color of each object is always seen in light. And 418b so we shall have first to explain what light is.

There is, then, we assume, something transparent; and by this I mean that which, though visible, is not properly speaking, visible in itself, but by reason of extrinsic color. Air, water, and many solid bodies answer to this description. For they are not transparent *quâ* air or *quâ* water, but because there is a certain natural attribute present in both of them which is present also in the eternal body on high. Light is the actuality of this transparent *quâ* transparent. But where the transparent is only potentially present, there darkness is actually. Light is a sort of color in the transparent when made transparent in actuality by the agency of fire or something resembling the celestial body: for this body also has an attribute which is one and the same with that of fire. What the transparent is, and what light is, has now been stated; namely, that it is neither fire nor body generally nor an effluence from any body (for even then it would still be a sort of body), but the presence of fire or something fiery in the transparent. For it is impossible for two bodies to occupy the same space at the same time.

Light is held to be contrary to darkness. But darkness

is absence from the transparent of the quality above described: so that plainly light is the presence of it. Thus Empedocles and others who propounded the same view are wrong when they represent light as moving in space and arriving at a given point of time between the earth and that which surrounds it without our perceiving its motion. For this contradicts not only the clear evidence of reason, but also the facts of observation: since, though a movement of light might elude observation within a short distance, that it should do so all the way from east to west is too much to assume.

It is that which is colorless which is receptive of color, as it is that which is soundless which is receptive of sound. And the transparent is colorless, and so is the invisible or the dimly visible which is our idea of the dark. Such is the transparent medium, not indeed when it is in actuality, but when potentially transparent. For it is the same natural attribute which is at one time darkness and at another time light. It is not everything visible which is visible in light, but only the proper color of each thing. Some things, indeed, are not seen in daylight, though they produce sensation in the dark: as, for example, the things of fiery and glittering appearance, for which there is not one distinguishing name, like fungus, horn, the heads, scales, and eyes of fishes. But in no one of these cases is the proper color seen. Why these objects are seen must be discussed elsewhere. At present this much is clear, that the object seen in light is color, and this is why it is not seen without light. For the very quiddity of color is, as we saw, just this, that it is capable of exciting change in the operantly transparent medium: and the activity of the transparent is light. There is clear evidence of this. If you lay the colored object upon your eye, you will not see it. On the contrary, what the color excites is the transparent medium, say, the

419a

air, and by this, which is continuous, the sense-organ is stimulated. For it was a mistake in Democritus to suppose that if the intervening space became a void, even an ant would be distinctly seen, supposing there were one in the sky. That is impossible. For sight takes place through an affection of the sensitive faculty. Now it cannot be affected by that which is seen, the color itself: therefore it can only be by the intervening medium: hence the existence of some medium is necessary. But, if the intermediate space became a void, so far from being seen distinctly, an object would not be visible at all.

We have explained the reason why color must be seen in light. fire is visible both in light and in darkness: and necessarily so, for it is owing to fire that the transparent becomes transparent. The same argument holds for sound and odor. For no sound or scent produces sensation by contact with the sense-organ: it is the intervening medium which is excited by sound and odor and the respective sense-organs by the medium. But, when the body which emits the sound or odor is placed on the sense-organ itself, it will not produce any sensation. The same holds of touch and taste, although it appears to be otherwise. The reason for this will be seen hereafter. The medium for sounds is air, that for odor has no name. For there is assuredly a common quality in air and water, and this quality, which is present in both, stands to the body which emits odor in the same relation as the transparent to color. For the animals that live in water also appear to have the sense 419b of smell. But man and the other land-animals which breathe are unable to smell without inhaling breath. The reason for this, too, must be reserved for future explanation.

8.   Let us now begin by determining the nature of sound and hearing. There are two sorts of sound, one a sound

which is operant, the other potential sound. For some things we say have no sound, as sponge, wool; others, for example, bronze and all things solid and smooth, we say have sound, because they can emit sound, that is, they can produce actual sound between the sonorous body and the organ of hearing. When actual sound occurs it is always of something on something and in something, for it is a blow which produces it. Hence it is impossible that a sound should be produced by a single thing, for, as that which strikes is distinct from that which is struck, that which sounds sounds upon something. And a blow implies spatial motion. As we stated above, it is not concussion of any two things taken at random which constitutes sound. Wool, when struck, emits no sound at all, but bronze does, and so do all smooth and hollow things; bronze emits sound because it is smooth, while hollow things by reverberation produce a series of concussions after the first, that which is set in motion being unable to escape. Further, sound is heard in air and, though more faintly, in water. It is not the air or the water, however, which chiefly determine the production of sound: on the contrary, there must be solid bodies colliding with one another and with the air: and this happens when the air after being struck resists the impact and is not dispersed. Hence the air must be struck quickly and forcibly if it is to give forth sound; for the movement of the striker must be too rapid to allow the air time to disperse: just as would be necessary if one aimed a blow at a heap of sand or a sandwhirl, while it was in rapid motion onwards.

Echo is produced when the air is made to rebound backwards like a ball from some other air which has become a single mass owing to its being within a cavity which confines it and prevents its dispersion. It seems likely that echo is always produced, but is not always distinctly audible:

since surely the same thing happens with sound as with light. For light is always being reflected; else light would not be everywhere, but outside the spot where the sun's rays fall there would be darkness. But it is not always reflected in the same way as it is from water or bronze or any other smooth surface; I mean, it does not always produce the shadow, by which we define light.

Void is rightly stated to be the indispensable condition of hearing. For the air is commonly believed to be a void, and it is the air which causes hearing, when being one and continuous it is set in motion. But, owing to its tendency to disperse, it gives out no sound unless that which is struck is smooth. In that case the air when struck is simultaneously reunited because of the unity of the surface; for a smooth body presents a single surface.

420a

That, then, is resonant which is capable of exciting motion in a mass of air continuously one as far as the ear. There is air naturally attached to the ear. And because the ear is in air, when the external air is set in motion, the air within the ear moves. Hence it is not at every point that the animal hears, nor that the air passes through: for it is not at every point that the part which is to set itself in motion and to be animate has a supply of air. Of itself, then, the air is a soundless thing because it is easily broken up. But, whenever it is prevented from breaking up, its movement is sound. But the air within the ears has been lodged fast within walls to make it immoveable, in order that it may perceive exactly all the varieties of auditory movement. This is why we hear in water also, because the water does not pass right up to the air attached to the ear, nor even into the ear at all, because of its convolutions. Should this happen, hearing is destroyed, as it is by an injury to the membrane of the tympanum, and as sight is by an injury to the cornea. Further, we have evidence whether we hear or not, according as there is or is not always a ringing sound in the ears, as in a horn: for the air imprisoned there is always moving with a proper motion of its own. But sound is something of external origin and is not native to the ear. And this is why it is said that we hear by means of what is empty and resonant, because that by which we hear has air confined within it.

Does that which is struck emit the sound or that which strikes? Is it not rather both, but each in a different way? For sound is motion of that which is capable of being moved in the same manner as things rebound from smooth surfaces when struck sharply against them. Thus, as above remarked, it is not everything which, when struck or striking, emits sound: supposing, for instance, a pin were to strike against a pin, there would be no sound. The thing struck must be of even surface, so that the air may rebound and vibrate in one mass.

The varieties of resonant bodies are clearly distinguished by the sound they actually emit. For, as without light colors are not seen, so without sound we cannot distinguish high and low or acute and grave in pitch. These latter terms are used by analogy from tangible objects. For the acute, that is, the high, note moves the sense much in a little time, while the grave' or low note moves it little in much time. Not that what is shrill is identically rapid, not what is low is slow, but it is in the one case the rapidity, in the other the slowness, which makes the motion or sensation such as has been described. And it would seem that there is a certain analogy between the acute and grave to the ear   420b
and the acute and blunt to the touch. For that which is acute or pointed, as it were, stabs, while the blunt, as it were, thrusts, because the one excites motion in a short, the other in a long time, so that *per accidens* the one is quick, the other slow. Let this account of sound suffice.

Voice is a sound made by an animate being. No inanimate thing is vocal, though it may by analogy be said
to be vocal, as in the case of the pipe, the lyre, and all
other inanimate things that have pitch and tune and
articulation: for these qualities, it would seem, the voice
also possesses. But many animals have no voice: that is
to say, all bloodless animals and, among animals that have
blood, fishes. And this is what we might expect, since sound
is a movement of air. Those fishes which are said to possess
voice, such as those in the Achelöus, merely make a noise
with their gills or some other such part. Voice is sound
made by an animal, and not by any part of its body in-
differently. But, as in every case of sound there is something
that strikes, something struck, and a medium, which is
air, it is reasonable that only creatures which inhale air
should have voice. For here nature uses the air that is
inhaled for two purposes, just as it uses the tongue for
tasting and for speech, the former use, for tasting, being
indispensable and therefore more widely found, while
expression of thought is a means to well-being. Similarly
nature uses the breath first as a necessary means to the
maintenance of internal warmth (the reason for which shall
be explained elsewhere) and, further, as a means of producing voice and so promoting well-being. The organ of
respiration is the larynx, and the part to which this part
is subservient is the lung: for it is this organ, namely, the
lung, which enables land animals to maintain a higher
temperature than others. Respiration is also needed primarily for the region about the heart. Hence, as we draw
breath, the air enters: and so the impact upon the windpipe,
as it is called, of the air breathed is voice, the cause of
the impact being the soul which animates the vocal organs.
For, as we said before, it is not every sound made by
an animal that is voice. Noise can be produced even with

the tongue or as in coughing: but it is necessary for voice
that the part which strikes should be animate and that
some mental image should be present. For voice is certainly
a sound which has significance and is not like a cough,
the noise of air respired: rather with this air the animal
makes the air in the windpipe strike against the windpipe.   421a
A proof of this is the fact that we cannot speak while
inhaling or exhaling breath, but only while we hold it in:
for anyone who holds his breath uses the breath so held
to cause motion. And it is evident why fishes are voiceless.
It is because they have no larynx. And they are without
this part because they do not take in the air nor breathe.
Why this is so does not concern us here.

9. Of smell and the object of smell it is less easy to speak
definitely than of the senses above-mentioned: for the nature
of odor is by no means so clear as is the nature of sound
or of color. The reason is that this sense in us is not exact,
but inferior to that of many animals. In fact, man has
a poor olfactory sense and perceives none of the objects
of smell unless they be painful or pleasant, which implies
that the organ is wanting in accuracy. It is reasonable to
suppose that animals with hard eyes perceive color in the
same vague way and do not distinguish the varieties of
color except in so far as they do, or do not, inspire fear.
And this is the way in which mankind perceive odors. For
it would seem that, while there is an analogy to taste and
the varieties of flavor answer to the varieties of smell, our
sense of taste is more exact because it is a modification
of touch and the sense of touch is the most exact of man's
senses. In the other senses man is inferior to many of the
animals, but in delicacy of touch he is far superior to the
rest. And to this he owes his superior intelligence. This
may be seen from the fact that it is this organ of sense

and nothing else which makes all the difference in the human race between the natural endowments of man and man. For hard-skinned men are dull of intellect, while those who are soft-skinned are gifted.

As with flavors, so with odors: some are sweet, some bitter. (But in some objects smell and flavor correspond; for example, they have sweet odor and sweet flavor: in other things the opposite is the case.) Similarly, too, an odor may be pungent, irritant, acid, or oily. But because, as we said above, odors are not as clearly defined as the corresponding flavors, it is from these latter that the odors have taken their names, in virtue of the resemblance in the things. Thus the odor of saffron and honey is sweet, while the odor of thyme and the like is pungent; and so in all the other cases. Again, smell corresponds to hearing and to each of the other senses in that, as hearing is of the audible and inaudible, and sight of the visible and invisible, so smell is of the odorous and inodorous. By inodorous may be meant either that which is wholly incapable of having odor or that which has a slight or faint odor. The term tasteless involves a similar ambiguity.

421b

Further, smell also operates through a medium, namely, air or water. For water animals, too, whether they are, or are not, possessed of blood, seem to perceive odor as much as the creatures in the air: since some of them also come from a great distance to seek their food, guided by the scent.

Hence there is an obvious difficulty, if the process of smell is everywhere the same, and yet man smells when inhaling but does not smell when instead of inhaling he is exhaling or holding his breath, no matter whether the object be distant or near, or even if it be placed on the inside of the nostril. The inability to perceive what is placed immediately on the sense-organ man shares with all animals:

what is peculiar to him is that he cannot smell without inhaling. This is made plain by experiment. Consequently bloodless animals, since they do not breathe, might be thought to have a distinct sense other than those commonly recognized. But, we reply, that is impossible, since it is odor which they perceive. For perception of odor, be it fragrant or noisome, constitutes smelling. Moreover, it is found that these bloodless animals are destroyed by the same powerful odors as man, such as asphalt, brimstone, and the like. It follows then that they do smell, but not by inhaling breath.

It would seem, again, that in man the organ of this sense differs from that of the other animals, as his eyes differ from those of hard-eyed animals. Man's eyes have, in the eyelids, a sort of screen or sheath and without moving or opening them he cannot see: while the hard-eyed animals have nothing of the kind, but at once see whatever is taking place in the transparent medium. So, too, it seems, the organ of smell in some animals is unenclosed, just as is the eye, but in those which take in the air it has a curtain, 422a which is removed in the process of inhaling, by dilatation of the veins and passages. And this is the reason why animals which breathe cannot smell in the water. For it is necessary for them to take in breath before smelling and this they cannot do in the water. Odor is included under that which is dry, as flavor under that which is moist, and the organ of smell is potentially dry also.

10. The object of taste is a species of tangible. And this is the reason why it is not perceived through a foreign body as medium: for touch employs no such medium either. The body, too, in which the flavor resides, the proper object of taste, has the moist, which is something tangible, for its matter or vehicle. Hence, even if we lived in water,

we should still perceive anything sweet thrown into the
water, but our perception would not have come through
the medium, but by the admixture of sweetness with the
fluid, as is the case with what we drink. But it is not in
this way, namely, by admixture, that color is perceived,
nor yet by emanations. Nothing, then, corresponds to the
medium; but to color, which is the object of sight, corresponds the flavor, which is the object of taste. But nothing
produces perception of flavor in the absence of moisture,
but either actually or potentially the producing cause must
have liquid in it: salt, for instance, for that is easily dissolved
and acts as a dissolvent upon the tongue.

Again, sight is of the invisible as well as the visible
(for darkness is invisible and this, too, sight discerns as
well as light) and, further, of that which is exceedingly
bright, which is likewise invisible, though in a different
way from darkness. Similarly hearing has to do with noise
and silence, the former being audible, the latter inaudible,
and, further, with loud noise, to which it is related as vision
is to brightness, a loud and a violent sound being in a
manner just as inaudible as a faint sound. The term invisible,
be it noted, is applied not only to that which it is wholly
impossible to see, which corresponds to other cases of the
impossible, but also when a thing has imperfectly or not
at all its natural properties, answering to the footless and
the kernel-less. So, too, taste has for object not only that
which can be tasted, but also the tasteless, by which we
mean that which has little flavor or hardly any at all, or
a flavor destructive of the taste. Now in flavor this distinction is supposed to start with the drinkable and the un-
drinkable. Both are tastes of a sort, but the latter is poor
or destructive of the faculty of taste, while the former is
naturally adapted to it. The drinkable is the common object
of touch and of taste. But, since the object of taste is moist,

the sense-organ which perceives it must be neither actually moist nor yet incapable of becoming moist. For taste is acted upon by the object of taste as such. The organ of taste, then, which needs to be moistened, must have the capacity of absorbing moisture without being dissolved, while at the same time it must not be actually moist. A proof of this is the fact that the tongue has no perception either when very dry or very moist. In the latter case the contact is with the moisture originally in the tongue, just as when a man first makes trial of a strong flavor and then tastes some other flavor; or as with the sick, to whom all things appear bitter because they perceive them with their tongue full of bitter moisture.

As with the colors, so with the species of flavor, there are, firstly, simple flavors, which are opposites, the sweet and the bitter; next to these on one side the succulent, on the other the salt; and, thirdly, intermediate between these, the pungent, the rough, the astringent, and the acid. These seem to be practically all the varieties of flavor. Consequently, while the faculty of taste has potentially the qualities just described, the object of taste converts the potentiality into actuality.

11. The same account is to be given of touch and the tangible. If touch is not a single sense but includes more senses than one, there must be a plurality of tangible objects also. It is a question whether touch is several senses or only one. What, moreover, is the sense-organ for the faculty of touch? Is it the flesh or what is analogous to this in creatures that have not flesh? Or is flesh, on the contrary, the medium, while the primary sense-organ for the faculty of touch? Is it the flesh or what is analogous to this in creatures that have not flesh? Or is flesh, on the contrary, the medium, while the primary sense-organ is something

different, something internal? We may argue thus: every sense seems to deal with a single pair of opposites, sight with white and black, hearing with high and low pitch, taste with bitter and sweet; but under the tangible are included several pairs of opposites, hot and cold, dry and moist, hard and soft, and the like. A partial solution of this difficulty lies in the consideration that the other senses also apprehend more than one pair of opposites. Thus in vocal sound there is not only high and low pitch, but also loudness and faintness, smoothness and roughness, and so on. In regard to color also there are other similar varieties. But what the one thing is which is subordinated to touch as sound is to hearing is not clear.

423a   But is the organ of sense internal or is the flesh the immediate organ? No inference can be drawn, seemingly, from the fact that the sensation occurs simultaneously with contact. For even under present conditions, if a sort of membrane were constructed and stretched over the flesh, this would immediately on contact transmit the sensation as before. And yet it is clear that the organ of sense is not in this membrane; although, if by growth it became united to the flesh, the sensation would be transmitted even more quickly. Hence it appears that the part of the body in question, that is, the flesh, is related to us as the air would be if it were united to us all round by natural growth. We should then have thought we were perceiving sound, color, and smell by one and the same instrument: in fact, sight, hearing, and smell would have seemed to us in a manner to constitute a single sense. But as it is, owing to the media, by which the various motions are transmitted, being separated from us, the difference of the organs of these three senses is manifest. But in regard to touch this point is at present obscure.

In fact, the animate body cannot consist of air or water

singly, it must be something solid. The only alternative is that it should be a compound of earth and of these elements, as flesh and what is analogous to flesh profess to be. Consequently the body must be the naturally cohering medium for the faculty of touch, through which the plurality of sensations is communicated. That they are a plurality is made clear by touch in the case of the tongue, for the tongue perceives all tangible objects, and that at the same part at which it perceives flavor. Now, if the rest of the flesh also had perception of flavor, taste and touch would have seemed to be one and the same sense: whereas they are really two, because their organs are not interchangeable.

Here a question arises. All body has depth, this being the third dimension, and, if between two bodies a third body is interposed, the two cannot touch one another. Now that which if fluid is not independent of body, nor is that which is wet: if it is not itself water, it must contain water. But when bodies touch one another in the water, since their exterior surfaces are not dry, there must be water between them, the water with which their extremities are flooded. If, then, all this be true, no one thing can possibly touch another in the water, nor yet in the air: for the air stands to the objects in the air as water to the things in water, but this fact we are more apt to overlook, just as aquatic animals fail to notice that the things which touch one another in the water have wet surfaces. The question 423b then arises: is the mode of perception uniform for all objects or does it differ for different objects? According to the prevalent view, taste and touch operate by direct contact, while the other senses operate at a distance. But this view is incorrect. On the contrary, we perceive the hard and the soft also mediately, just as much as we do the resonant, the visible, the odorous. But the latter are perceived at a distance, the former close at hand: and this is why the fact escapes us, since we really perceive all objects through a medium, though in touch and taste we fail to notice this. And yet, as we mentioned above, even if we perceived all objects of touch through a membrane without being aware of its interference, we should be just in the same position as we are now with regard to objects in the water or in the air: for, as it is, we suppose that we are touching the objects themselves and that there is no intervening medium. But there is this difference between the tangible on the one hand and visible and resonant things on the other: the latter we perceive because the medium acts in a certain way upon us, while tangible objects we perceive not by any action upon us of the medium, but concurrently with it, like the man who is struck through his shield. It is not that the shield was first struck and then passed on the blow, but, as it happened, both were struck simultaneously. And, generally, it would seem that the flesh and the tongue are related to the true sense-organ as are air and water to the organs of sight, hearing, and smell respectively. But neither in the one case nor in the other would sensation follow on contact with the sense-organ; for instance, if a body that is white were placed on the outer surface of the eye: which shows that the instrument that apprehends the tangible is within. We should then get the same result as in the case of the other senses. What is placed on the sense-organ we do not perceive: what is placed on the flesh we do perceive: therefore flesh is the medium for the faculty of touch.

It is, then, the distinctive qualities of body as body which are the objects of touch: I mean those qualities which determine the elements, hot or cold, dry or moist, of which we have previously given an account in our discussion of the elements. And their sense-organ, the tactile organ, that is, in which the sense called touch primarily resides, is the part which has potentially the qualities of the tangible object. For perceiving is a sort of suffering or being acted upon: 424a so that when the object makes the organ in actuality like itself it does so because that organ is potentially like it. Hence it is that we do not perceive what is just as hot or cold, hard or soft, as we are, but only the excesses of these qualities: which implies that the sense is a kind of mean between the opposite extremes in the sensibles. This is why it passes judgment on the things of sense. For the mean is capable of judging, becoming to each extreme in turn its opposite. And, as that which is to perceive white and black must not be actually either, though potentially both, and similarly for the other senses also, so in the case of touch the organ must be neither hot nor cold. Further, sight is in a manner, as we saw, of the invisible as well as the visible, and in the same way the remaining senses deal with opposites. So, too, touch is of the tangible and the intangible: where by intangible is meant, first, that which has the distinguishing quality of things tangible in quite a faint degree, as is the case with the air; and, secondly, tangibles which are in excess, such as those which are positively destructive. Each of the senses, then, has now been described in outline.

12. In regard to all sense generally we must understand that sense is that which is receptive of sensible forms apart from their matter, as wax receives the imprint of the signet ring apart from the iron or gold of which it is made: it takes the imprint which is of gold or bronze, but not *quâ* gold or bronze. And similarly sense as relative to each sensible is acted upon by that which possesses color, flavor, or sound, not in so far as each of those sensibles is called a particular thing, but in so far as it possesses a particular quality and in respect of its character or form. The primary

sense-organ is that in which such a power resides, the power to receive sensible forms. Thus the organ is one and the same with the power, but logically distinct from it. For that which perceives must be an extended magnitude. Sensitivity, however, is not an extended magnitude, nor is the sense: they are rather a certain character or power of the organ. From this it is evident why excesses in the sensible objects destroy the sense-organs. For if the motion is too violent for the sense-organ, the character or form (and this, as we saw, constitutes the sense) is annulled, just as the harmony and the pitch of the lyre suffer by too violent jangling of the strings. It is evident, again, why plants have no sensation, although they have one part of soul and are in some degree affected by the things themselves which are tangible: for example, they become cold and hot. The reason is that they have in them no mean, no principle capable of receiving the forms of sensible objects without their matter, but on the contrary, when they are acted upon, the matter acts upon them as well. It might be asked whether what is unable to smell would be in any way acted upon by an odor, or that which is incapable of seeing by a color, and so for the other sensibles. But, if the object of smell is odor, the effect it produces, if it produces an effect at all, is smelling. Therefore none of the things that are unable to smell can be acted upon by odor, and the same is true of the other senses: nor can things be acted upon when they have the power of sensation, except as they individually possess the particular sense required. This may also be shown as follows. Light and darkness do not act upon bodies at all; neither does sound nor odor: it is the things which possess them that act. Thus it is the air accompanying the thunderbolt which rives the timber. But, it may be said, things tangible and flavors do so act: else by what agency are inanimate things acted upon or changed? Shall we,

424b

then, conclude that the objects of the other senses likewise act directly? Is it not rather the case that not all body can be affected by smell and sound, and that the bodies which are so affected are indeterminate and shifting; for example, air? For odor in the air implies that the air has been acted upon in some way. What then is smelling besides a sort of suffering or being acted upon? Or shall we say that the act of smelling implies sense-perception, whereas the air, after it has been acted upon, so far from perceiving, at once becomes itself perceptible to sense?

BOOK III

1. That there is no other sense distinct from the five, by which I mean sight, hearing, smell, taste, touch, anyone may convince himself on the following grounds. Let us assume that, as a matter of fact, we have sensation of every sensible object for which touch is the appropriate sense, all qualities of the tangible, as such, being perceptible to us through touch. Let us further assume that, when any sense is lacking to us, an organ of sense must also be lacking; and further, that whatever we perceive by actual contact is perceptible by touch, a sense which we do possess, while whatever we perceive mediately and not by actual contact is perceptible by means of the elements, namely, air and water. And here are implied two cases. Suppose, first, we have perception by one and the same medium of two several things, different in kind from one another, then whoever possesses the appropriate sense-organ must be percipient of both: as, for example, if the sense-organ consists of air and air is also the medium of both sound and color. Next

425a suppose several media to transmit the same object, as both
air and water transmit color, both being transparent, then
he who possesses one of these alone will perceive whatever
is perceptible through both media. Now, of the elements,
air and water are the only two of which sense-organs are
composed. For the pupil of the eye is of water, and the
ear is of air, and the organ of smell is of one or the other,
while fire, if present anywhere, enters into all, since nothing
can be sentient without warmth. Earth, again, belongs to
none of the sense-organs, or, at most, is a constituent
peculiar to touch. It follows, then, that outside water and
air there is no sense-organ. Now sense-organs composed
of air and water certain animals do, in fact, possess. We
may infer, then, that all the senses are possessed by those
animals which are fully developed and are not crippled:
even the mole is found to have eyes beneath its skin. And
thus, unless there exists some unknown body or some
property different from any possessed by any of the bodies
within our experience, there can be no sixth sense which
we lack.

Nor, again, can there be ay special sense-organ for
the common sensibles, which we perceive incidentally by
every sense; for example, motion, rest, figure, magnitude,
number, unity. For all of these we perceive by motion.
Thus it is by motion that we perceive magnitude, and
consequently figure, figure being one variety of magnitude;
while that which is at rest we perceive by the fact that
it is not moved. Number we perceive by the negation of
continuity and by the special sense-organs also: for each
sensation has a single object. Clearly, then, it is impossible
that there should be a special sense for any one of these;
for example, motion: for in that case we should perceive
them in the same way as we now perceive sweetness by
sight (and this we do because we have a sense which per-

ceives both, and by this we actually apprehend the two simultaneously when they occur in conjunction). Otherwise we should never have more than an incidental perception of them; as of Cleon's son we perceive not that he is Cleon's son, but that he is a white object, and the fact of his being Cleon's son is accessory to the whiteness. But of the common sensibles we have already a common perception, which is direct and not indirect, so that there cannot be a special sense for them. For, if there were, we should never perceive them otherwise than in the way in which we said we saw Cleon's son.

But the various senses incidentally perceive each other's proper objects, not as so many separate senses, but as forming a single sense, when there is concurrent perception relating to the same object; as, for instance, when we perceive that gall is bitter and yellow. For it is certainly not the part of any other sense to declare that both objects are one and the same. Hence you are sometimes deceived and, on observing something yellow, fancy it to be gall.

But, it might be asked, why have we several senses, instead of only one? I answer, it is in order that we may not be so likely to overlook the common attributes, such as motion, magnitude, number, which accompany the special sensibles. For, if sight had been our only sense and whiteness its object, we should have been more apt to overlook the common sensibles and to confuse all sensibles, because color and magnitude, for instance, must always go together. As it is, the fact that the common attributes are found in the object of another sense also shows that they are severally distinct.

2.   Inasmuch as we perceive that we see and hear, it must either be by sight or by some other sense that the percipient perceives that he sees. But, it may be urged, the same sense

425b

which perceives sight will also perceive the color which
is the object of sight. So that either there will be two senses
to perceive the same thing or the one sense, sight, will
perceive itself. Further, if the sense perceiving sight were
really a distinct sense, either the series would go on to
infinity or some one of the series of senses would perceive itself. Therefore it will be better to admit this of the
first in the series. Here, however, there is a difficulty. Assuming that to perceive by sight is to see and that it is
color or that which possesses color which is seen, it may
be argued that, if you are to see that which sees, that which
in the first instance sees, the primary visual organ, will
actually have color. Clearly, then, to perceive by sight does
not always mean one and the same thing. For, even when
we do not see, it is nevertheless by sight that we discern
both darkness and light, though not in the same manner.
Further, that which sees is in a manner colored. For the
sense-organ is in every case receptive of the sensible object
without its matter. And this is why the sensations and images
remain in the sense-organs even when the sensible objects
are withdrawn.

Now the actuality of the sensible object is one and
the same with that of the sense, though, taken in the abstract,
sensible object and sense are not the same. I mean, for
example, actual sound and actual hearing are the same:
for it is possible to have hearing and yet not hear; again,
that which is resonant is not always sounding. But when
that which is capable of hearing operantly hears and that
which is capable of sounding sounds, the actual hearing
and the actual sound occur simultaneously, and we might,
if we pleased, call them audition and resonance respectively.
If, then, motion, action, and passivity reside in that which
is acted upon, then of necessity it is in the potentiality
of hearing that there is actual sound and there is actual

426a

hearing. For the activity of agent and movement comes into play in the patient; and this is why that which causes motion need not itself be moved. The actuality of the resonant, then, is sound or resonance, and the actuality of that which can hear is hearing or audition, hearing and sound both having two meanings. The same account may be given of the other senses and their objects. For, just as acting and being acted upon are in the subject acted upon and not in the agent, so also the actuality of the sensible object and that of the sensitive faculty will be in the percipient subject. But in some cases both activities have a name; for example, resonance and audition: in other cases one or the other has no name. Thus, while the actuality of sight is called seeing, that of color has no name; and, while the actuality of the taste-faculty is called tasting, that of the flavor has no name. Now, as the actuality of the object and that of the faculty of sense are one and the same, although taken in the abstract they are different, hearing and sound thus understood as operant must simultaneously cease to be or simultaneously continue in being, and so also with flavor and taste, and similarly with the other senses and their objects: but when they are understood as potentialities, there is no such necessity. On this point the earlier natural philosophers were in error, when they supposed that without seeing there was neither white nor black, and without tasting no flavor. Their statement is in one sense true, in another false. For the terms sensation and sensible thing are ambiguous. When they mean the actual sensation and the actual sensible thing, the statement holds good: when they mean potential sensation and potential sensible, this is not the case. But our predecessors used terms without distinguishing their various meanings.

If, then, concord consists in a species of vocal sound, and if vocal sound and hearing are in one aspect one and the same [*though in another aspect not the same*], and if concord is a proportion, it follows that hearing must also be a species of proportion. And this is the reason why hearing is destroyed by either excess, whether of high pitch or of low. And similarly, in the case of flavors, excess destroys the taste, and in colors excessive brightness or darkness destroys the sight, and so with smell, whether the excessive odor be agreeable or pungent. All this implies that the sense is a proportion. Hence sensibles are, it is true, pleasurable when they are brought into the range of this proportion pure and unmixed; for example, the shrill, the sweet, the salt: in that case, I say, they are pleasurable. But, speaking generally, that in which ingredients are blended is pleasurable in a higher degree, accord more pleasurable to the ear than high pitch or low pitch alone, and to touch that which admits of being still further heated or cooled. The due proportion constitutes the sense, while objects in excess give pain or cause destruction.

426b

Now each sense is concerned with its own sensible object, being resident in the organ, *quâ* sense-organ, and judges the specific differences of its own sensible object. Thus sight pronounces upon white and black, taste upon sweet and bitter, and so with the rest. But, since we compare white and sweet and each of the sensibles with each, what in fact is it by means of which we perceive the difference between them? It must be by sense, for they are sensibles. And thus it is clear that the flesh is not the ultimate organ of sense; for, if it were, it would be necessary that that which judges should judge by contact with the sensible object. Nor indeed can we with separate organs judge that sweet is different from white, but both objects must be clearly presented to some single faculty. For, if we could, then the mere fact of my perceiving one thing and your perceiving another would make it clear that the two things were different. But the single faculty is required to pronounce them different, for sweet and white are pronounced to be different. It is one and the same faculty, then, which so pronounces. Hence, as it pronounces, so it also thinks and perceives. Clearly, then, it is not possible with separate organs to pronounce judgment upon things which are separate: nor yet at separate times, as the following considerations show. For, as it is one single faculty which pronounces that good and bad are different, so when it judges "*A* is different from *B*" it also judges "*B* is different from *A*" (and in this case the "when" is not accidental; I mean, accidental in the sense in which I may now say "Such and such things are different" without saying that they are different now. On the contrary, it pronounces now and pronounces that *A* and *B* are different now). That which judges judges, then, instantaneously and hence as an inseparable unit in an inseparable time. But, again, it is impossible for the same thing, insofar as indivisible and affected in indivisible time, to be moved at the same instant with contrary motions. For, if the object be sweet, it moves sense or thought in such and such a way, but what is bitter moves it in a contrary way, and what is white in a different way. Is, then, that which judges instantaneous in its judgment and numerically undivided and inseparable, although separate logically? Then it is in a certain sense that which is divided which perceives divided objects; in another sense it is *quâ* indivisible that the divided perceives them: that is to say, logically it is divisible, locally and numerically it is indivisible. Or is this impossible? For the same indivisible unity, though in potentiality each of two opposites, in the order of thought and being is not so, but in actual operation is divided: it is impossible that it should be at the same time both white and black, and hence impossible that it should receive at the same time the forms of white and

427a

black, if reception of the forms constitutes sensation and thought. Rather is the case parallel to that of the point, as some describe it, which is divisible insofar as it is regarded as one or two. Well then, in so far as the faculty which judges is indivisible, it is one and judges instantaneously; but, in so far as it is divisible, it is not one, for it uses the same point at the same time twice. So far as it treats the boundary-point as two, it passes judgment on two separate things with a faculty which in a manner is separated into two; so far as it treats the point as one, it passes judgement on one thing, and that instantaneously. So much, then, for the principle in virtue of which we call the animal capable of sensation.

3. There are two different characteristics by which the soul is principally defined; firstly, motion from place to place and, secondly, thinking and judging and perceiving. Both thought and intelligence are commonly regarded as a kind of perception, since the soul in both of these judges and recognizes something existent. The ancients, at any rate, identify intelligence and perception: thus, in the words of Empedocles: "Wisdom for mankind is increased according to that which is present to them": and again "Whence they have also continually a shifting succession of thoughts." Homer's meaning, too, is the same when he says: "Such is the mind of men." In fact, all of them conceive thought to be corporeal like sensation and hold that we understand, as well as perceive, like by like: as we explained at the outset of the discussion. They ought, however, at the same time to have discussed error, a state which is peculiarly characteristic of animal life and in which the soul continues the greater part of its time. It follows from their premises that either all presentations of the senses must be true, as some affirm, or contact with what is unlike must con-

427b

stitute error; this being the converse of the position that like is known by like. But, as the knowledge of contraries is one and the same, so, too, it would seem, is error with respect to contraries one and the same. Now it is clear that perception and intelligence are not the same thing. For all animals share in the one, but only a few in the other. And when we come to thinking, which includes right thinking and wrong thinking, right thinking being intelligence, knowledge, and true opinion, and wrong thinking the opposites of these, neither is this identical with perception. For perception of the objects of the special senses is always true and is found in all animals, while thinking may be false as well as true and is found in none which have not reason also. Imagination, in fact, is something different both from perception and from thought, and is never found by itself apart from perception, any more than is belief apart from imagination. Clearly thinking is not the same thing as believing. For the former is in our own power, whenever we please: for we can represent an object before our eyes, as do those who range things under mnemonic headings and picture them to themselves. But opining is not in our power, for the opinion that we hold must be either false or true. Moreover, when we are of opinion that something is terrible or alarming, we at once feel the corresponding emotion, and so, too, with what is reassuring. But when we are under the influence of imagination we are no more affected than if we saw in a picture the objects which inspire terror or confidence. There are also different forms even of belief; knowledge, opinion, intelligence and their opposites. But the difference between these species must be reserved for another discussion.

To turn to thought: since it is different from sense-perception and seems to include imagination on the one

hand and conception on the other, we must determine the
nature of imagination before we proceed to discuss conception. If, then, imagination is the faculty in virtue of
428a   which we say that an image presents itself to us, and if
we exclude the metaphorical use of the term, it is some
one of the faculties or habits in virtue of which we judge,
and judge truly or falsely. Such faculties or habits are
sensation, opinion, knowledge, intellect. It is clearly not
sensation, for the following reasons. Sensation is either a
faculty like sight or an activity like seeing. But we may
have an image even when neither the one nor the other
is present: for example, the images in dreams. Again, sensation is always present, but not so imagination. Besides,
the identity of the two in actuality would involve the possibility that all the brutes have imagination. But this apparently is not the case; for example, the ant, the bee, and
the grub do not possess it. Moreover, sensations are always
true, but imaginings prove for the most part false. Further, it is not when we direct our energies closely to the
sensible object, that we say that this object appears to us
to be a man, but rather when we do not distinctly perceive
it [then the term true or false is applied]. And, as we said
before, visions present themselves even if we have our eyes
closed.

Neither, again, can imagination be ranked with the
faculties, like knowledge or intellect, which always judge
truly: it may also be false. It remains, then, to consider
whether it be opinion, as opinion may be true or false.
But opinion is attended by conviction, for it is impossible
to hold opinions without being convinced of them: but
no brute is ever convinced, though many have imagination. Further, every opinion implies conviction, conviction
implies that we have been persuaded, and persuasion implies reason. Among brutes, however, though some have

imagination, none have reason. It is evident, then, that imagination is neither opinion joined with sensation nor opinion through sensation, nor yet a complex of opinion and sensation, both on these grounds and because nothing else is the object of opinion but that which is the object of sensation: I mean, it is the complex of the opinion of white and the sensation of white, which alone could constitute imagination. To imagine, then, will be on this supposition to opine directly, not indirectly, that which we perceive. But there are false imaginings concerning things   428b of which we hold at the same time a true conception. For example, the sun appears only a foot in diameter, but we are convinced that it is larger than the inhabited world: in this case, therefore, either, without any alteration in the thing and without any lapse of memory on our part or conversion by argument, we have abandoned the true opinion which we had about it; or else, if we still retain it, the same opinion must be both true and false. It could have proved false only in the event of the object having changed without our observing it. It is not, then, either one of the two, opinion and sensation, singly, or a combination of the two, which constitutes imagination.

Now when one thing is moved, something else can be moved by it. And imagination is thought to be a species of motion and not to rise apart from sensation, but only in sentient beings and with the objects of sense for its objects. Motion, again, may be produced by actual sensation, and such motion must resemble the sensation which caused it. From all this it follows that this particular motion cannot arise apart from sensation nor be found anywhere except in sentient beings: and in virtue of this motion it is possible for its possessor to do and experience many things: imagination, too, may be both true and false. The reasons for the last conclusion are as follows. Perception of the objects of the special senses is true, or subject to the minimum of error. Next comes the perception that they are attributes: and at this point error may come in. As to the whiteness of an object sense is never mistaken, but it may be mistaken as to whether the white object is this thing or something else. Thirdly, there is perception of the common attributes, that is, the concomitants of the things to which the special attributes belong: I mean, for example, motion and magnitude, which are attributes of sensibles. And it is concerning them that sense is most apt to be deceived. But the motion which is the result of actual sensation will be different according as it arises from one or other of these three kinds of perception. The first kind, so long as the sensation is present, is true: the other kinds may be false, whether the sensation is present or absent, and especially when the object perceived is a long way off. If then, imagination possesses no other characteristics than the aforesaid, and if it is what it has been described to be, imagination will be a motion generated by actual perception. And, since sight is the principal sense, imagination has derived even its name (φαντασία) from light (φάος), because without light one cannot see. Again, because imaginations remain in us and resemble the corresponding sensations, animals perform many actions under their influence; some, that is, the brutes, through not having intellect, and others, that is, men, because intellect is sometimes obscured by passion or disease or sleep. Let this account of the nature and cause of imagination suffice.

429a

4.   As to the part of the soul with which it knows and understands, whether such part be separable spatially, or not separable spatially, but only in thought, we have to consider what is its distinctive character and how thinking comes about. Now, if thinking is analogous to perceiving,

it will consist in a being acted upon by the object of thought or in something else of this kind. This part of the soul, then, must be impassive, but receptive of the form and potentially like this form, though not identical with it: and, as the faculty of sense is to sensible objects, so must intellect be related to intelligible objects. The mind, then, since it thinks all things, must needs, in the words of Anaxagoras, be unmixed with any, if it is to rule, that is, to know. For by intruding its own form it hinders and obstructs that which is alien to it; hence it has no other nature than this, that it is a capacity. Thus, then, the part of the soul which we call intellect (and by intellect I mean that whereby the soul thinks and conceives) is nothing at all actually before it thinks. Hence, too, we cannot reasonably conceive it to be mixed with the body: for in that case it would acquire some particular quality, cold or heat, or would even have some organ, as the perceptive faculty has. But as a matter of fact it has none. Therefore it has been well said that the soul is a place of forms or ideas: except that this is not true of the whole soul, but only of the soul which can think, and again that the forms are there not in actuality, but potentially. But that the impassivity of sense is different from that of intellect is clear if we look at the sense-organs and at sense. The sense loses its power to perceive, if the sensible object has been too intense: thus it cannot hear sound after very loud noises, and after too powerful colors and odors it can neither see nor smell. But the intellect, when it has been thinking on an object   429b
of intense thought, is not less, but even more, able to think of inferior objects. For the perceptive faculty is not in-dependent of body, whereas intellect is separable. But when the intellect has thus become everything in the sense in which one who actually is a scholar is said to be so (which happens so soon as he can exercise his power of himself),

even then it is still in one sense but a capacity; not, however, a capacity in the same sense as before it learned or discovered. And, moreover, at this stage intellect is capable of thinking itself.

Now, since magnitude is not the same as the quiddity of magnitude, nor water the same as the quiddity of water (and so also of many other things, though not of all, the thing and its quiddity being in some cases the same), we judge the quiddity of flesh and flesh itself either with different instruments or with the same instrument in different relations. For flesh is never found apart from matter, but, like "snub-nosed," it is a particular form in a particular matter. It is, then, with the faculty of sense that we discriminate heat and cold and all those qualities of which flesh is a certain proportion. But it is with another faculty, either separate from sense, or related to it as the bent line when it is straightened out is related to its former self, that we discriminate the quiddity of flesh. Again, when we come to the abstractions of mathematics, the straight answers to the quality "snub-nosed," being never found apart from extension. But the straightness of that which is straight, always supposing that the straight is not the same as straightness, is something distinct: we may, for instance, assume the definition of straightness to be duality. It is, then, with another instrument or with the same instrument in another relation that we judge it. In general, therefore, to the separation of the things from their matter corresponds a difference in the operations of the intellect.

The question might arise: assuming that the mind is something simple and impassive and, in the words of Anaxagoras, has nothing in common with anything else, how will it think, if to think is to be acted upon? For it is in so far as two things have something in common that the one of them is supposed to act and the other

to be acted upon. Again, can mind itself be its own object? For then either its other objects will have mind in them, if it is not through something else, but in itself, that mind in them, if it is not through something else, but in itself, that mind is capable of being throught, and if to be so capable is everywhere specifically one and the same; or else the mind will have some ingredient in its composition which makes it, like the rest, an object of thought. Or shall we recall our old distinction between two meanings of the phrase "to be acted upon in virtue of a common element," and say that the mind is in a manner potentially all objects of thought, but is actually none of them until it thinks: potentially in the same sense as in a tablet which has nothing actually written upon it the writing exists   430a
potentially? This is exactly the case with the mind. Moreover, the mind itself is included among the objects which can be thought. For where the objects are immaterial that which thinks and that which is thought are identical. Speculative knowledge and its object are identical. (We must, however, inquire why we do not think always.) On the other hand, in things containing matter each of the objects of thought is present potentially. Consequently material objects will not have mind in them, for the mind is the power of becoming such objects without their matter; whereas the mind will have the attribute of being its own object.

5.   But since, as in the whole of nature, to something which serves as matter for each kind (and this is potentially all the members of the kind) there corresponds something else which is the cause or agent because it makes them all, the two being related to one another as art to its material, of necessity these differences must be found also in the soul. And to the one intellect, which answers to this descrip-

tion because it becomes all things, corresponds the other because it makes all things, like a sort of definite quality such as light. For in a manner light, too, converts colors which are potential into actual colors. And it is this intellect which is separable and impassive and unmixed, being in its essential nature an activity. For that which acts is always superior to that which is acted upon, the cause or principle to the matter. Now actual knowledge is identical with the thing known, but potential knowledge is prior in time in the individual; and yet not universally prior in time. But this intellect has no intermittence in its thought. It is, however, only when separated that it is its true self, and this, its essential nature, alone is immortal and eternal. But we do not remember because this is impassive, while the intellect which can be affected is perishable and without this does not think at all.

6.   The process of thinking indivisible wholes belongs to a sphere from which falsehood is excluded. But where both truth and falsehood are possible there is already some combining of notions into one. As, in the words of Empedocles, "where sprang into being the neckless heads of many creatures," then afterwards Love put them together, so these notions, first separate, are combined; as, for instance, the notions incommensurable and diagonal. And, if the thinking refers to the past or to the future, the notion of time is included in the combination. Falsehood, in fact, never arises except when notions are combined. For, even if white be asserted to be not-white, not-white is brought into a combination. We may equally well call every statement a disjunction. But at any rate under truth and falsehood we include not only the assertion that Cleon is white, but also the assertion that he was or will be. And the unifying principle is in every case the mind.

430b

Since, however, the term indivisible has two meanings, according as a whole is not potentially divisible or is actually undivided, there is nothing to hinder us from thinking an indivisible whole, when we think of a length (that being actually undivided), or from thinking it in an indivisible time. For the time is a divisible or indivisible unit in the same way as the length thought of. We cannot therefore state what the mind thinks in each half of the time. For, if the whole be undivided, the half has only potential existence. But, if the mind thinks each half separately, it simultaneously divides the time also. And in that case it is as if the parts were separate lengths. If, however, the mind conceives the length as made up of the two halves, then the time may be regarded as made up of corresponding halves.

Again, that which is not quantitatively but specifically an indivisible whole the mind thinks in an indivisible unit of time and by an indivisible mental act. *Per accidens,* however, such specific unity is divisible, though not in the same way as they, the act of thought and the time required for the act, are divisible, but in the same way as they are whole and indivisible. For in these specific unities also there is present a something indivisible, though certainly not separately existent, the same as that which constitutes the unity of both the time and the length. And, as with time and length, so in like manner with whatever is continuous. But the point and every division and whatever is an undivided whole in the same sense as the point is clearly explained by the analogy of privation. And the same explanation holds in all other cases. How, for instance, is evil apprehended, or black? In some fashion by its contrary. But that which apprehends must potentially be, and must contain within itself, the contrary which it apprehends. If, however, there be something which has no contrary [*some one of the causes*], then it is itself the content of its own knowledge, is in actuality and is separately existent.

431a Now every proposition, like an affirmative proposition, predicating something of something, is true or false. But with thought this is not always so. When its object is the What in the sense of the quiddity and there is no predication, thought is in every case true. But, as the perception by sight of the proper object of sight is infallibly true, whereas in the question whether the white object is a man or not, perception by sight is not always true, so is it with immaterial objects.

7. Now actual knowledge is identical with the thing known. But potential knowledge is prior in time in the individual, and yet not universally prior even in time. For it is from something actually existent that all which comes into being is derived. And manifestly the sensible object simply brings the faculty of sense which was potential into active exercise: in this transition, in fact, the sense is not acted upon or qualitatively changed. Consequently this must be a different species of motion. For motion is, as we saw, an activity of that which is imperfect; but activity in the absolute sense, that is, activity of that which has reached perfection, is quite distinct.

Sensation, then, is analogous to simple assertion or simple apprehension by thought and, when the sensible thing is pleasant or painful, the pursuit or avoidance of it by the soul is a sort of affirmation or negation. In fact, to feel pleasure or pain is precisely to function with the sensitive mean, acting upon good or evil as such. It is in this that actual avoidance and actual appetition consist: nor is the appetitive faculty distinct from the faculty of avoidance, nor either from the sensitive faculty; though logically they are different. But to the thinking soul images serve as present sensations: and when it affirms or denies good or evil, it avoids or pursues (this is why the soul never thinks without an image). To give an illustration: the air impresses a certain quality on the pupil of the eye, and this in turn upon something else, and so also with the organ of hearing, while the last thing to be impressed is one and is a single mean, though with a plurality of distinct aspects.

What that is by which the soul judges that sweet is different from warm has been explained above, but must be restated here. It is a unity, but one in the same sense as a boundary point, and its object, the unity by analogy of these two sensibles or their numerical unity, is related to each of the two in turn as they, taken separately, are to each other. For what difference does it make whether we ask how we judge the sensibles that do not fall under the same genus, or the contraries which do, like white and black? Suppose, then, that as *A,* the white, is to *B,* the black, so *C* is to *D* [*that is, as those sensibles are to one another*]. It follows, *convertendo,* that *A* is to *C* as *B* to *D.* If, then, *C* and *D* are attributes of a single subject, the relation between them, like that between *A* and *B,* will be that they are one and the same, though the aspects they present are distinct: and so, too, of their single subject. The same would hold, supposing *A* were the sweet and *B* the white.   431b

Thus it is the forms which the faculty of thought thinks in mental images. And, as in the region of sense the objects of pursuit and avoidance have been defined for it, so also outside sensation, when engaged with images, it is moved to action: as, for instance, you perceive a beacon and say "That is fire"; and then [*by the central sense*], seeing it in motion, you recognize that it signals the approach of an enemy. But at other times under the influence of the

images or thoughts in the soul you calculate as though
you had the objects before your eyes and deliberate about
the future in the light of the present. And when you pronounce, just as there in sensation you affirm the pleasant
or the painful, here in thought you pursue or avoid: and
so in action generally. And, further, what is unrelated to
action, as truth and falsehood, is in the same class with
the good and the evil. Yet in this, at any rate, they differ,
that the former are absolute, the latter relative to some
one concerned.

But the abstractions of mathematics, as they are called,
the mind thinks as it might conceive the snub-nosed; *quâ*
snub-nosed, it would not be conceived apart from flesh,
whereas *quâ* hollow, if anyone ever had actually so conceived it, he would have conceived it without the flesh in
which the hollowness resides. So, too, when we think of
mathematical objects, we conceive them, though not in fact
separate from matter, as though they were separate. And,
speaking generally, mind in active operation is its objects
[*when it thinks them*]. The question, whether it is possible
for the mind to think anything which is unextended without
being itself unextended, must for the present be postponed.

8.   And now let us sum up what has been said concerning
the soul by repeating that in a manner the soul is all existent
things. For they are all either objects of sensation or objects
of thought; and knowledge and sensation are in a manner
identical with their respective objects. How this is so requires
to be explained. Knowledge and sensation, then, are sub-
divided to correspond to the things. Potential knowledge
and sensation answer to things which are potential, actual
knowledge and sensation to things which are actual, while
the sensitive and the cognitive faculties in the soul are
potentially these objects; I mean, object of sensation and

object of cognition respectively. It follows that the faculties must be identical, if not with the things themselves, then with their forms. The things themselves they are not, for it is not the stone which is in the soul, but the form of the stone. So that there is an analogy between the soul and the hand; for, as the hand is the instrument of instruments, so the intellect is the form of forms and sensation the form of sensibles. But, since, apart from sensible magnitudes there is nothing, as it would seem, independently existent, it is in the sensible forms that the intelligible forms exist, both the abstractions of mathematics, as they are called, and all the qualities and attributes of sensible things. And for this reason, as without sensation a man would not learn or understand anything, so at the very time when he is actually thinking he must have an image before him. for mental images are like present sensations, except that they are immaterial. Imagination, however, is distinct from affirmation and negation, for it needs a combination of notions to constitute truth or falsehood. But, it may be asked, how will the simplest notions differ in character from mental images? I reply that neither these nor the rest of our notions are images, but that they cannot dispense with images.

432a

9.   The soul in animals has been defined in virtue of two faculties, not only by its capacity to judge, which is the function of thought and perception, but also by the local movement which it imparts to the animal. Assuming the nature of sensation and intellect to have been so far determined, we have now to consider what it is in the soul which initiates motion: whether it is some one part of the soul, which is either locally separable or logically distinct, or whether it is the whole soul: and again, if a separate part, whether it is a special part distinct from those usually

recognized and from those enumerated above, or whether it coincides with some one of these. A question at once arises in what sense it is proper to speak of parts of the soul and how many there are. For in one sense there appear to be an infinite number of parts and not merely those which some distinguish, the reasoning, passionate, and concupiscent parts, for which others substitute the rational and the irrational. For, if we examine the differences on which they base their divisions, we shall find that there are other parts separated by a greater distance than these; namely, the parts which we have just discussed, the nutritive, which belongs to plants as well as to all animals, and the sensitive, which cannot easily be classed either as rational or irrational. Imagination, again, is logically distinct from them all, while it is very difficult to say with which of 432b the parts it is in fact identical or not identical, if we are to assume separate parts in the soul. Then besides these there is appetency, which would seem to be distinct both in concept and in capacity from all the foregoing. And surely it is absurd to split this up. For wish in the rational part corresponds to concupiscence and passion in the irrational. And, if we make a triple division of soul, there will be appetency in all three parts.

To come now to the question at present before us, what is it that imparts to the animal local movement? For as for the motion of growth and decay, which is found in all animals, it would seem that this must be originated by that part of soul which is found in all of them, the generative and nutritive part. Inspiration and expiration of breath, sleep and waking, subjects full of difficulty, call for subsequent inquiry. But to return to locomotion, we must inquire what it is that imparts to the animal progressive motion. That it is not the nutritive faculty is clear. For this motion is always directed to an end and is attended either by imagination or by appetency. No animal, which is not either seeking or avoiding something, moves except under compulsion. Moreover, if it were the nutritive faculty, plants also would be capable of locomotion and thus would have some part instrumental in producing this form of motion. Similarly it is not the sensitive faculty, since there are many animals which have sensation and yet are throughout their lives stationary and motionless. If, then, nature does nothing in vain and, except in mutilated and imperfect specimens, omits nothing that is indispensable, while the animals we are considering are fully developed and not mutilated—as is shown by the fact that they propagate their kind and have a period of maturity and a period of decline,—it follows that, if locomotion was implied in sensation, they would have had the parts instrumental to progression. Nor, again, is it the reasoning faculty or what is called intellect that is the cause of motion. For the speculative intellect thinks nothing that is practical and makes no assertion about what is to be avoided or pursued, whereas motion always implies that we are avoiding or pursuing something. But, even if the mind has something of the kind before it, it does not forthwith prompt avoidance or pursuit. For example, it often thinks of something alarming or pleasant without prompting to fear; the only effect is a beating of the heart or, when the thought is pleasant, some other bodily movement. Besides, even if the intellect issues the order and the understanding bids us avoid or pursue something, still we are not thereby moved to act: on the contrary, action is determined by desire; in the case, for instance, of the incontinent man. And generally we see that, although a man possesses a knowledge of medicine, it does not follow that he practices; and this implies that there is something else apart from the knowledge which determines action in accordance with the knowledge. Nor,

433a

again, is it solely appetency on which this motion depends. The continent, though they feel desire, that is appetite, do not act as their desires prompt, but on the contrary obey reason.

10. The motive causes are apparently, at any rate, these two, either appetency or intelligence, if we regard imagination as one species of thinking. For men often act contrary to knowledge in obedience to their imaginings, while in the other animals there is no process of thinking or reasoning, but solely imagination. Both these, then, are causes of locomotion, intelligence, and appetency. By intelligence we mean that which calculates the means to an end, that is, the practical intellect, which differs from the speculative intellect by the end at which it aims. Appetency, too, is directed to some end in every case: for that which is the end of desire is the starting point of the practical intellect, and the last stage in this process of thought is the starting point of action. Hence there is good reason for the view that these two are the causes of motion, appetency, and practical thought. For it is the object of appetency which causes motion; and the reason why thought causes motion is that the object of appetency is the starting point of thought. Again, when imagination moves to action, it does not move to action apart from appetency. Thus there is one single moving cause, the appetitive faculty. For, had there been two, intelligence and appetency, which moved to action, still they would have done so in virtue of some character common to both. But, as a matter of fact, intellect is not found to cause motion apart from appetency. For rational wish is appetency; and, when anyone is moved in accordance with reason, he is also moved according to rational wish. But appetency may move a man in opposition to reason, for concupiscence is a species of appetency. While,

however, intellect is always right, appetency and imagination may be right or wrong. Hence it is invariably the object of appetency which causes motion, but this object may be either the good or the apparent good. Not all good, however, but practical good: where by practical good we mean something which may not be good under all circumstances.

It is evident, then, that motion is due to the faculty of the soul corresponding to this object—I mean what is known as appetency. But those who divide the soul into parts, if they divide it according to its powers and separate these from one another, will find that such parts tend to become very numerous: nutritive, sensitive, intelligent, deliberative, with the further addition of an appetent part: for these differ more widely from one another than the concupiscent does from the passionate. Now desires arise which are contrary to one another, and this occurs whenever reason and the appetites are opposed, that is, in those animals which have a perception of time. For intelligence bids us resist because of the future, while appetite has regard only to the immediate present; for the pleasure of the moment appears absolutely pleasurable and absolutely good because we do not see the future. Therefore, while generically the moving cause will be one, namely, the faculty of appetency, as such, and ultimately the object of appetency (which, without being in motion itself, causes motion by the mere fact of being thought of or imagined), numerically there is a plurality of moving causes.

Now motion implies three things, first, that which causes motion, secondly, that whereby it causes motion, and again, thirdly, that which is moved; and of these that which causes motion is twofold, firstly, that which is itself unmoved and, secondly, that which both causes motion and is itself moved. The unmoved movement is the practical

433b

good, that which is moved and causes motion is the appetitive faculty (for the animal which is moved is moved in so far as it desires, and desire is a species of motion or activity) and, finally, the thing moved is the animal. But the instrument with which desire moves it, once reached, is a part of the body: hence it must be dealt with under the functions common to body and soul. For the present, it may be enough to say summarily that we find that which causes motion by means of organs at the point where beginning and end coincide; as, for instance, they do in the hinge-joint, for there the convex and the concave are respectively the end and the beginning, with the result that the latter is at rest, while the former moves, convex and concave being logically distinct, but locally inseparable. For all animals move by pushing and pulling, and accordingly there must be in them a fixed point, like the center in a circle, and from this the motion must begin. Thus, then, in general terms, as already stated, the animal is capable of moving itself just in so far as it is appetitive: and it cannot be appetitive without imagination. Now imagination may be rational or it may be imagination of sense. Of the latter the other animals also have a share.

11. We must also consider what is the moving cause in those imperfect animals which have only the sense of touch. Is it possible that they should have imagination and desire, or is it not? It is evident that they feel pleasure and pain: and, if they have these, then of necessity they must also feel desire. But how can they have imagination? Shall we say that, as their movements are vague and indeterminate, so, though they have these faculties, they have them in a vague and indeterminate form? The imagination of sense, then, as we have said, is found in the other animals also, but deliberative imagination in those alone which have

434a

reason.—For the task of deciding whether to do this or that already implies reasoning. And the pursuit of the greater good necessarily implies some single standard of measurement. Hence we have the power of constructing a single image out of a number of images.—And the reason why the lower animals are thought not to have opinion is that they do not possess that form of imagination which comes from inference, while the latter implies the former. And so appetency does not imply the deliberative faculty. But sometimes it overpowers rational wish and moves to action; at other times the latter, rational wish, overpowers the former, appetency. Thus one appetency prevails over another appetency, like one sphere over another sphere, in the case where incontinence has supervened. But by nature the upper sphere always has the predominance and is a moving cause, so that the motion is actually the resultant of three orbits.

The cognitive faculty, however, is not subject to motion, but is at rest. The major premiss is universal, whether judgment or proposition, while the minor has to do with a particular fact: for, while the former asserts that such and such a person ought to do such and such an act, the latter asserts that a particular act is one of the sort and that I am such a person. Now it is the latter judgment which at once moves to action, not the universal. Or shall we say that it is both together, but the one is akin to the unmoved movement, the other is not?

12. Every living thing, then, must have the nutritive soul and in fact has a soul from its birth till its death. For what has been born must necessarily grow, reach maturity, and decline, and for these processes nutriment is indispensable. It follows, then, of necessity that the nutritive faculty is present in all things that grow and decay. But sensation is not necessarily present in all living things. For

wherever the body is uncompounded there can be no sense of touch [*yet without this sense animal existence is impossible*]: nor, again, in those living things which are incapable of receiving forms apart from matter. But the animal must of necessity possess sensation, if nature makes nothing in vain: for everything in nature subserves an end or else will be an accessory of things which subserve an end. Now every living body having the power of progression and yet lacking sensation would be destroyed and never reach full development, which is its natural function. For how in such a case is it to obtain nutriment? Motionless animals, it is true, have for nutriment that from which they have been developed. But a body, not stationary, but produced by generation, cannot possibly have a soul and an intelligence capable of judging without also having sensation. [*Neither can it, if it be not generated.*] For why should it have the one without the other? Presumably for the advantage either of the soul or of the body. But neither of these alternatives is, in fact, admissible. For the soul will be no better able to think, and the body will be no better off, for the absence of sensation. We conclude, then, that no body that is not stationary has soul without having sensation.

434b

But, further, the body, assuming that it has sensation, must be either simple or composite. But it cannot be simple, for then it would not have touch, and this sense is indispensable. This is clear from the following considerations. The animal is an animate body. Now body is always tangible and it is that which is perceptible by touch which is tangible: from which it follows that the body of the animal must have tactile sensation, if the animal is to survive. For the other senses, that is to say, smell, sight, hearing, have media of sensation, but a being which has no sensation will be unable when it comes into contact with things to avoid some and seize others. And if this is so, it will be impossible for the animal to survive. This is why taste is a kind of touch, for taste is of nutriment and nutriment is body which is tangible; whereas sound, color, and smell afford no nourishment and promote neither growth nor decay. So that taste also must be a kind of touch, because it is a sensation of that which is tangible and nutritive. These two senses, then, are necessary to the animal, and it is plain that without touch no animal can exist.

But the other senses are means to well-being, and are necessary, not to any and every species of animal, but only to certain species, as, for example, those capable of loco-motion. For, if the animal capable of locomotion is to survive, it must have sensation, not only when in contact with anything, but also at a distance from it. And this will be secured if it can perceive through a medium, the medium being capable of being acted upon and set in motion by the sensible object, and the animal itself by the medium. Now that which causes motion from place to place produces a change operating within certain limits, and that which propels causes the thing propelled to propel in turn, the movement being transmitted through something interme-diate. The first in the series initiates motion and propels without being itself propelled, while the last is simply pro-pelled without propelling; the numerous middle terms of the series both propel and are propelled. So it is also with qualitative change, except that what is subject to this change   435a
remains in the same place. Suppose we were to dip some-thing into wax, the movement in the wax would extend just so far down as we had dipped the object, whereas in the like case a stone is not moved at all, while water is disturbed to a great distance and air is disturbed to the farthest extent possible and acts and is acted upon as long as it remains unbroken. And, to revert to the reflection

of light, that is why, instead of holding that the visual ray leaving the eye is reflected, it would be better to say that the air is acted upon by the shape and color, so long as it is one and unbroken. This is the case over any smooth surface: and accordingly the air acts on the organ of sight in turn, just as if the impress on the wax had penetrated right through to the other side.

13. It is evident that the body of an animal cannot be uncompounded; I mean, it cannot consist entirely of fire, for instance, or of air. An animal, unless it has touch, can have no other sense, the animate body being always, as we have remarked, capable of tactile sensation. Now the other elements, with the exception of earth, would make sense-organs: but it is always indirectly and through media that such organs effect sensation. Touch, however, acts by direct contact with objects: hence its name. The other sense-organs, it is true, also perceive by contact, but it is by indirect contact: touch alone, it would seem, perceives directly in and through itself. Thus, then, no one of the three elements referred to can constitute the body of the animal. Nor indeed can it be of earth. For touch is a sort of mean between all tangible qualities, and its organ is receptive not only of all the distinctive qualities of earth, but also of heat and cold and all other tangible qualities. And this is why we do not perceive anything with our bones and our hair and such parts of us, namely, because they are of earth. And for the same reason plants, too, have no sensation, because they are composed of earth.

435b Without touch, however, there can be no other sense; and the organ of this sense does not consist of earth nor of any other single element.

Thus it is evident that this is the only sense the loss of which necessarily involves the death of the animal. For it is not possible for anything that is not an animal to have this sense, nor is it necessary for anything that is an animal to have any other sense besides this. And this explains another fact. The other sensibles—I mean, color, sound, odor—do not by their excess destroy the animal, but only the corresponding sense-organs: except incidentally, as when concurrently with the sound some thrust or blow is given, or when objects of sight or smell move something else which destroys by contact. Flavor, again, destroys only in so far as it is at the same time tactile. Tangible qualities, on the other hand, as heat, cold, and hardness, if in excess, are fatal to the living animal. For excess of any sensible object is fatal to the organ, and so consequently excess of the tangible object is fatal to touch. And it is by this sense that the life of the animal is defined, touch having been proved to be indispensable to the existence of an animal. Hence excess in tangible qualities destroys not only the sense-organ, but also the animal itself. For touch is the one sense that the animal cannot do without. The other senses which it possesses are, as we have said, the means, not to its being, but to its well-being. Thus the animal has sight to see with, because it lives in air or water or, speaking generally, in a transparent medium. It has taste on account of what is pleasant and painful, to the end that it may perceive what is pleasant in food and feel desire and be impelled to movement. It has hearing in order that information may be conveyed to it, and a tongue, that in its turn it may convey information to its fellow.

COSIMO is a specialty publisher of books and publications that inspire, inform, and engage readers. Our mission is to offer unique books to niche audiences around the world.

COSIMO BOOKS publishes books and publications for innovative authors, nonprofit organizations, and businesses. **COSIMO BOOKS** specializes in bringing books back into print, publishing new books quickly and effectively, and making these publications available to readers around the world.

COSIMO CLASSICS offers a collection of distinctive titles by the great authors and thinkers throughout the ages. At **COSIMO CLASSICS** timeless works find new life as affordable books, covering a variety of subjects including: Business, Economics, History, Personal Development, Philosophy, Religion & Spirituality, and much more!

COSIMO REPORTS publishes public reports that affect your world, from global trends to the economy, and from health to geopolitics.

FOR MORE INFORMATION CONTACT US AT
INFO@COSIMOBOOKS.COM

❋ if you are a book lover interested in our current catalog of books

❋ if you represent a bookstore, book club, or anyone else interested in special discounts for bulk purchases

❋ if you are an author who wants to get published

❋ if you represent an organization or business seeking to publish books and other publications for your members, donors, or customers.

**COSIMO BOOKS ARE ALWAYS
AVAILABLE AT ONLINE BOOKSTORES**

VISIT COSIMOBOOKS.COM
BE INSPIRED, BE INFORMED

CPSIA information can be obtained at www.ICGtesting.com
Printed in the USA
LVOW080821230612

287210LV00001B/58/P

9 781605 204321